Memories
of
Reading

Part of the

Memories

series

*The Publishers would like to thank the following companies for supporting
the production of this book*

Main Sponsor

Scottish Courage Brewing Limited

Alan Hadley Limited

Haslams Chartered Surveyors

Hicks Developments Limited

E Jackson and Sons Limited

A F Jones

Rowberry Morris

First published in Great Britain by True North Books Limited
Units 3 - 5 Heathfield Industrial Park
Elland West Yorkshire
HX5 9AE
Tel. 01422 377977
© Copyright: True North Books Limited 1999

ISBN 1 900463 49 0

Text, design and origination by True North Books Limited
Printed and bound by The Amadeus Press Limited

Memories are made of this

Memories. We all have them; some good, some bad, but our memories of the town we grew up in are usually tucked away in a very special place in our minds. The best are usually connected with our childhood and youth, when we longed to be grown up and paid no attention to adults who told us to enjoy being young, as these were the best years of our lives. We look back now and realise that they were right.

So many memories - perhaps of the war and rationing, perhaps of parades, celebrations and royal visits. And so many changes; one-way traffic systems and pedestrianisation. New trends in shopping that led to the very first self-serve stores being opened.

Through the bad times and the good, however, Reading not only survived but prospered. We have only to look at the town as it is today, to see what progress has been realised and what achievements have been made over the last 50 years. Reading has a history to be proud of - but more importantly, a great future to look forward to, into the new millennium and beyond.

Contents

Around the town centre

Rain on the cobbles, drizzle in the air - the words 'damp and dreary' spring to mind when describing the kind of day it was when a photographer set up his equipment to record for posterity the demolition of Holmes' store. It was 1932, and traffic levels in the town had grown to such an extent that plans were afoot to widen St Mary's Butts - the start of the vast changes which were eventually to transform the old street. Today, Broad Street Mall, with its many shops, cafes and modern car park, has replaced the buildings on the right, including the White Hart hotel which would have been a new building at the time of this photograph;

the Virgin Megastore was to stand on the site by the 1990s. The White Hart was a Simonds house - the local brewery set up by William Blackall Simonds in the late 19th century using a legacy from his father. With his change to banking in the 1830s, William's son Blackall Simonds carried on building up the brewery business - which was eventually to be taken over by Courage.

St Mary's Butts owes its unusual name to the weekly archery practice which took place at the archery butts in medieval times - a compulsory duty imposed on all able bodied men 'in defence of the realm'.

Events of the 1930s

HOT OFF THE PRESS

The years of the 1930s saw Adolf Hitler's sickening anti-Jewish campaign echoed in the streets of Britain. On 19th October 1936 Oswald Mosley's 7,000-strong British Union of Fascists clashed head on with thousands of Jews and Communists in London, resulting in 80 people being injured in the ensuing battle. Mosley and his 'blackshirts' later rampaged through the streets beating up Jews and smashing the windows of their businesses.

GETTING AROUND

At the beginning of the decade many believed that the airship was the transport of the future. The R101 airship, however, loaded with thousands of cubic metres of hydrogen, crashed in France on its maiden flight in 1930. Forty-eight passengers and crew lost their lives. In 1937 the Hindenburg burst into flames - the entire disaster caught on camera and described by a distraught reporter. The days of the airship were numbered.

SPORTING CHANCE

In 1939 British racing driver Sir Malcolm Campbell hit the headlines when he captured the world's water-speed record for the third time in 'Bluebird' - all his cars were given the same name. A racing driver who set world speed records both on land and on water, Sir Malcolm established world land-speed records no fewer than nine times. His son Donald went on to set further records, tragically dying in 1967 when his speedboat - also named 'Bluebird' - crashed.

Two-way traffic was still making its way along St Mary's Butts when this view was captured around 1930, though the pedestrians in the shot, some of whom appear to be making their way to or from the refreshment cabin (as today in the centre of the road), would seem to be in no immediate danger of becoming involved in a traffic accident! Few people had a telephone in their home in the 1930s, so these telephone boxes - an up to date facility in the town - would

have seen far less use than their modern counterparts today. How many readers remember the 'You may telephone from here' signs that were often mounted outside shops in places where there was no public phone box? Beyond the snack bar we can see the two-tiered fountain which was built to commemorate Queen Victoria's golden jubilee in 1887. The fountain was officially turned on by the Mayoress in June of that year, though today flowers have replaced the running water.

Since this photograph, Broad Street shopping mall has replaced buildings on the left, and The Pavlov's Dog pub, which has seen many name changes in recent years, now stands opposite the refreshment kiosk.

Left: 'Our stock must be cleared! Wonderful Bargains!' shouts the huge notice outside Holmes & Sons store, and the sign also makes clear the reason for the sale: 'Road widening scheme'. We can see how much narrower St Mary's Butts was at the time of the photograph in 1932, and the demolition of properties on the right (the original White Hart also went) gave us the wide road we know today. Looking around for some traffic to direct was the good old bobby on point duty (where did they all go to?); note the four-footed transport among the motor vehicles in the scene, bringing to mind those gentler days when noise from the town's traffic involved only the rattle of wheels and the clip-clop of hooves, and the only traffic pollution could be put to good use on your floribunda! Horse-drawn carts, especially popular among coal merchants and milkmen, were with us right into the 1940s and even in some places the 50s.

Below: There was a time when every major junction in every major town had its traffic 'bobby', though this officer, stationed at the junction of Broad Street, West Street and St Mary's Butts, was not overburdened with work, there being more pedestrians than cars in this shot. Point duty must have demanded a high concentration of manpower, however, and it was no doubt argued that instead of directing the town's traffic the police force would be better employed in concentrating their efforts on the fight against crime. So a few at a time they departed, leaving the motorist with a legacy of traffic lights to contend with at each junction. The White Hart pub on the right was built in 1932 when the road was widened, and replaced an earlier pub of the same name. We must hope that the unlucky occupant of the pram parked outside and snapped by the photographer did not have to wait too long for his parents to quench what was obviously an overpowering thirst with a quick pint of Simonds!

A block of modern offices stands today where Loveridge's ironmongery business stood in this view of King Street, snapped in 1938. This was obviously the place where the householder, gardener and shopkeeper alike could stock up on their needs, whether they wanted to buy a pair of shop scales, have a lawn mower repaired, or buy a dozen galvanised nails and a set of cup hooks. Adjoining Loveridge's is a building which will be familiar to every reader - Barclays Bank. The impressive building, commissioned by Simonds brewers, was designed by Henry and Nathaniel Briant - and the original brass plate declaring this to be 'Simonds Bank' still remains on the door. The external view of the bank is, however, deceptive, as the Bath stone facade is the only part of the building which escaped the red pen of the developer. During the 1970s the interior was gutted and entirely modernised, and sadly no effort was made to harmonise with the original Victorian architecture. We can see that trams were still running in Reading at the time, and on this wet day few would be riding on the upper decks. The days of the old trams were already numbered, however, and the following year would see them withdrawn from service.

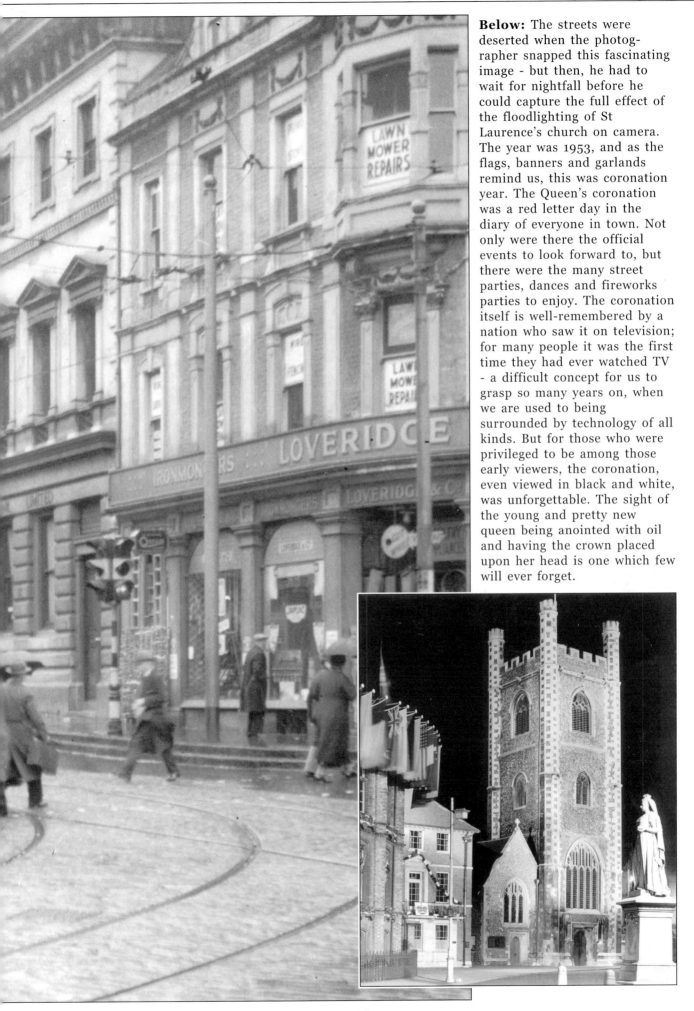

Below: The streets were deserted when the photographer snapped this fascinating image - but then, he had to wait for nightfall before he could capture the full effect of the floodlighting of St Laurence's church on camera. The year was 1953, and as the flags, banners and garlands remind us, this was coronation year. The Queen's coronation was a red letter day in the diary of everyone in town. Not only were there the official events to look forward to, but there were the many street parties, dances and fireworks parties to enjoy. The coronation itself is well-remembered by a nation who saw it on television; for many people it was the first time they had ever watched TV - a difficult concept for us to grasp so many years on, when we are used to being surrounded by technology of all kinds. But for those who were privileged to be among those early viewers, the coronation, even viewed in black and white, was unforgettable. The sight of the young and pretty new queen being anointed with oil and having the crown placed upon her head is one which few will ever forget.

It was a sunny day in 1960, perfect for photographing one of Reading's pleasant open spaces. Reading is fortunate to possess so many magnificent churches, but St Mary's is the town's oldest, and timbers that once formed part of Reading Abbey were incorporated into the church's roof. When the tower of St. Mary's was rebuilt, stone from the Abbey was used to create its familiar chequerboard pattern. Little remains of the 12th century abbey itself, which was consecrated in 1164 by St Thomas Becket, though its site once covered 30 acres of the town. Stone by stone, the ruined abbey was taken apart until the flint core of its walls were all that remained - though some of its stone carvings still survive. At one time the view St Mary's was blocked by cottages; to the relief of

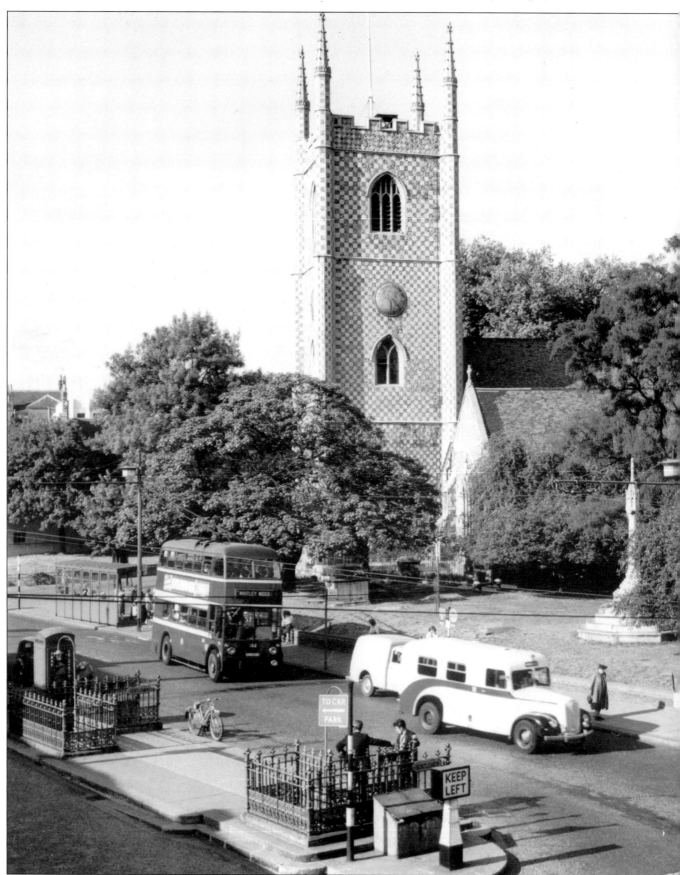

local people they were demolished in 1886, opening up the view of the church - which still impresses visitors with its beauty.

On a different note, the public loos in the foreground were an often much-appreciated part of Reading for many years. Public toilets often find their inglorious way into old photographs, and though these particular facilities have now closed down, interestingly the thick glass tiles set into the pavement above them still survive.

Events of the 1930s

SCIENCE AND DISCOVERY

By observing the heavens, astronomers had long believed that there in the constellation of Gemini lay a new planet, so far undiscovered. They began to search for the elusive planet, and a special astronomical camera was built for the purpose. The planet Pluto was discovered by amateur astronomer Clyde Tombaugh in 1930, less than a year later.

WHAT'S ON?

In this heyday of the cinema, horrified audiences were left gasping at the sight of Fay Wray in the clutches of the giant ape in the film 'King Kong', released in 1933. Very different but just as gripping was the gutsy 1939 American Civil War romance 'Gone with the Wind'. Gable's parting words, 'Frankly, my dear, I don't give a damn' went down in history. 1936 - Britain set up the world's first television service - black and white, of course. The Queen's coronation in 1953, the first such ceremony to be televised, did much to popularise television.

ROYAL WATCH

The talking point of the early 1930s was the affair of the Prince of Wales, who later became King Edward VIII, and American divorcee Wallis Simpson. Faced with a choice, Edward gave up his throne for 'the woman I love' and spent the remainder of his life in exile. Many supported him, though they might not have been as keen to do so if they had been aware of his Nazi sympathies, kept strictly under wraps at the time.

Below: The sixties were already swinging when this scene in the Market Place was recorded - the traffic system and the Market Place itself has changed somewhat since this Vauxhall Victor drove in the direction of Friar Street.
Was this an FB Victor or a VX490, we wonder? (The two models were virtually indistinguishable from the front.) Readers who were lucky enough to possess one might remember the unusual system which some FB Victors had, with a steering column mounted gearchange, three forward gears and reverse. The handbrake was of the pull-out variety, situated under the dashboard, and this meant that they could have a 'bench' seat in the front, running the full width of the car, American-style. This made the car seem very spacious, and combined with the real leather upholstery and lots of chrome, the de luxe model was luxury indeed!
The Simeon Monument behind the car has been part of Reading's history since 1804, when it was erected by the prominent local citizen Edward Simeon 'as a mark of affection for his native town'. The monument's simple lines could almost, we feel, have been produced by one of today's minimalist designers; its creator was Sir John Soane, architect of the Bank of England.

Right: The wearing of cycle helmets - a valuable addition to Britain's road safety guidelines - lay far in the future when this cyclist rode along Friar Street in 1961. Behind the hoardings lay what was at the time a construction site, and before long the building which was to become the British Telecom offices would rise skywards floor by floor. Many readers will remember the adjoining Blagrave Buildings, which would be the next old property to disappear from this scene. This not unpleasant Victorian building housed shops and stores on the ground floor, with residential flats above. Blagrave Buildings was demolished in 1962 when modernisation began in Friar Street.
It was a sunny summer day when this scene was recorded, and C & G Ayres, who occupied the premises on the right, were coal and coke merchants. As recently as the 1960s majority of households had open fires, which burnt one or the other. The firm would perhaps not be doing too well at the time of the photograph, as summer time would obviously be their slack period. Still, the cooler days of autumn lay just ahead, and business would soon be booming once again.

Wartime

Bright smiles on the faces of people with a serious job to do: this cheerful group of people are fire watchers who were stationed on the roof of the Town Hall - and it was there that they assembled for this commemorative group photograph, kindly donated by Miss M Swadling. During World War II everyone was called upon to play an active part in winning the war, and the people of Reading joined organisations, dug for victory, made do and mended their old clothes, and became fire watchers. The names of the men in the group are lost to us, though the ladies are (left to right) Miss M Swadling,

Miss P Reeves, Miss G Lambden and Miss Budds. The threat from incendiaries was a very real one, and on more than one occasion incendiaries had fallen into unattended office blocks and factories and started fires. A two-hour bombing raid on London just after Christmas in 1940 started a total of 1,500 fires, many of them burning unchecked in city centre properties. After that, firewatching became a compulsory duty, and all men between 16 and 60 were called on to organise a fire-watching rota. Later on women between 20 and 45 joined them.

This page: Those who are too young to remember the second world war will agree that it is amazing what havoc can be wreaked by a stick of four bombs. The covered arcade and the surrounding buildings caught the full blast of one of the bombs dropped in what was labelled a 'hit and run raid'.

Long before war was declared in 1939 preparations were going ahead for the conflict that many saw as inevitable. Reading, however, was not seen as a major target for enemy bombers, and so became a 'safe town' for refugees. Bombs did in fact fall during 1940 and 1941, destroying three houses in Cardiff Road, though a milkman's horse was the only fatality. But on 10th February 1943 a single Dornier made up for the early neglect of the town in one bombing run. Wellsteeds department store, offices in the Town Hall, St Laurence's church were also badly damaged, while the People's Pantry restaurant took a direct hit in the raid. During the years that followed the Great War, long range bombers had been developed, which meant that the second world war was the first war that held any real threat from the air. Both Britain and Germany now possessed aircraft which were capable of carrying large bomb loads and flying for long distances. The problem for towns in the Thames Valley was that they were situated just a few minutes' flying time from German air bases, and even in clear weather the long south of England coastline made it difficult to detect the approach of enemy planes. On that fatal day, by the time the single plane was detected, there was little time for air raid sirens to give warning. People were caught up in the raid before they had time to get to the shelters, and the German pilot machine-gunned them in the streets before dropping his four bombs across the town.

This page and overleaf: The faces of sadness - these two young women look utterly devastated as they contemplate the damage done in Reading's major bombing raid to Wellsteeds department store in Broad Street, which was to eventually become Debenhams *(right)*. Were they, perhaps, shop girls, saddened by the loss of the store - and possibly their jobs? It was the back of the well-known store that took the full force of the bomb, and if it had not been half day closing, casualties would have been very high. The day was brightened by the attitude of one very small hero; the local newspaper later reported that seven year old Clarence Brown had taken the raid in his stride, acting with a coolness and courage that many adults lacked. When he was pulled from the rubble by a group of soldiers, he quickly said 'I'm all right' - then pointed them to the spot where two women and a girl were buried. They were later rescued from the debris.

There was little left of the offices of Blandy & Blandy - their frontage was severely damaged and staff injured, and offices in the Town Hall were also reduced to a heap of rubble *(below and overleaf)*. St Laurence's church was also badly damaged;

Events of the 1930s

MELODY MAKERS

Throughout the 1930s a young American trombonist called Glenn Miller was making his mark in the world of music. By 1939 the Glenn Miller sound was a clear leader in the field; his clean-cut, meticulously executed arrangements of numbers such as 'A String of Pearls' and 'Moonlight Serenade' brought him fame across the world as a big-band leader. During a flight to England from Paris in 1944 Miller's plane disappeared; no wreckage was ever found.

THE WORLD AT LARGE

In India, Gandhi's peaceful protests against British rule were gathering momentum. The Salt Laws were a great bone of contention: forced to buy salt from the British government, thousands of protestors marched to the salt works, intending to take it over in the name of the Indian people. Policemen and guards attacked the marchers, but not one of them fought back. Gandhi, who earned for himself the name 'Mahatma' - Great Soul - was assassinated in 1948.

INVENTION AND TECHNOLOGY

With no driving tests or speed restrictions, 120,000 people were killed on the roads in Britain between the two world wars. In 1934 a Halifax man, Percy Shaw, invented a safety device destined to become familiar the world over: reflecting roadstuds. In dark or foggy conditions the studs that reflected light from the car's headlights kept traffic on the 'straight and narrow' and must over the years have saved many lives.

the raid blew out most of its fine stained glass windows, damaged the altar and scattered organ pipes around the church. Although the top of the church tower looks virtually untouched, the pinnacles were later found to be unsafe and had to be removed.

The war was long and hard, and by 1945 the people of Reading were

well and truly fed up with the privations of wartime Britain. When peace was declared after six long years of war, Winston Churchill announced, 'We have never seen a greater day than this.'

In Reading bunting was strung from house to house across every street and patriotic flags flapped gaily in the breeze, and along with the rest of Britain people found the energy to let their hair down and organise Victory Parades, street parties, fireworks displays and bonfires. At last it was time for hope, and time to start again.

Both pages: The premises of A R Saunders in Minster Street were badly damaged in the devastating air raid of Wednesday 10th February 1943, and window frames hang at a drunken angle among the shattered floorboards and collapsed masonry, while damaged roof timbers lie open to the air *(left)*. A daring fire fighter mounts a long extended ladder on his appliance to check on the damage. While Saunders lies half in ruins, their building was not, however, the worst casualty of the raid. It was getting on for tea time when the solitary bomber fixed his sights on Reading, and the People's Pantry restaurant in Friar Street was crowded with hungry workers enjoying a well-earned meal at the end of the day. The restaurant took a direct hit *(below)*, instantly burying both customers and staff in the ruins of the building. In what was by far Reading's worst raid of the entire war, rescue parties worked by torchlight to free victims from the rubble, though sadly many were already dead and the Air Raid Precautions personnel had the heartbreaking task of removing their bodies. The WVS were quickly on the scene, dishing out hot drinks to the Civil Defence workers; a hot mug of tea was often just what they needed as they battled with coolness and courage hour after hour in unbelievable conditions in their search for people who might be still alive in the ruins. A total of 41 people lost their lives in Reading's day of horror, and 49 sustained serious injuries. The King and Queen had endeared themselves in most places to air raid victims, and after the raid in Reading the Queen sent cards to everyone who was injured, together with a food hamper, which would no doubt have been very much appreciated.

Events of the 1940s

HOT OFF THE PRESS

At the end of World War II in 1945 the Allies had their first sight of the unspeakable horrors of the Nazi extermination camps they had only heard of until then. In January, 4,000 emaciated prisoners more dead than alive were liberated by the Russians from Auschwitz in Poland, where three million people, most of them Jews, were murdered. The following year 23 prominent Nazis faced justice at Nuremberg; 12 of them were sentenced to death for crimes against humanity.

THE WORLD AT LARGE

The desert area of Alamogordo in New Mexico was the scene of the first atomic bomb detonation on July 16, 1945. With an explosive power equal to more than 15,000 tons of TNT, the flash could be seen 180 miles away. President Truman judged that the bomb could secure victory over Japan with far less loss of US lives than a conventional invasion, and on 6th August the first of the new weapons was dropped on Hiroshima. Around 80,000 people died.

ROYAL WATCH

By the end of World War II, the 19-year-old Princess Elizabeth and her distant cousin Lieutenant Philip Mountbatten RN were already in love. The King and Queen approved of Elizabeth's choice of husband, though they realised that she was rather young and had not mixed with many other young men. The engagement announcement was postponed until the Princess had spent four months on tour in Africa. The couple's wedding on 20th November 1947 was a glittering occasion - the first royal pageantry since before the war.

Everyone loves a parade, especially if there is a rousing band to keep everyone in step, and on 4th June 1944 hundreds of local people turned out to watch this parade through Reading. The American Military Police present a fine sight as every one in step they march smartly past the mayor and civic dignitaries who were there to take the salute.

The Japanese attack on Pearl Harbor, which killed nearly 2,500, outraged Americans, and President Roosevelt declared it a 'day that

will live in infamy'. That same day, 8th December 1941, both Britain and the USA declared war on Japan. Before long, American troops set up bases around Britain, and the new and more flamboyant attitude of the newcomers helped to lighten the wartime mood in many places. The war brought together people who in the normal course of events would never have met, and romance blossomed between many British girls and American GIs.

During the second world war parades became an accepted part of British life; children loved the excitement of the stirring bands and the marching soldiers, and the processions undoubtedly made the average person in the street feel in touch with the military and the progress of the war. A year on, the town centre saw the culmination of all the years of struggle - the victory parade of May 1945.

Events & occasions

The Great War was just a year old when King George V and Queen Mary visited Reading on July 31st 1915, and the care of the injured and the sick was high on every agenda *(below)*. A hospital visit was a must for the royal couple, and a photographer caught this fascinating image of the procession of cars carrying their Majesties as the fleet was about to turn into the gates of the Royal Berkshire Hospital. We can see that small children have wormed their way to the front of the crowds that lined Oxford Road, and having obtained the best view in the house they wave and cheer for the King and Queen as enthusiastically as anyone else. Hats are being waved among the older people behind them, and if we were not aware that the month was July, the men's straw boaters and the ladies' light and pretty headgear would remind us that it was summer. The King was keenly interested in the war, visiting the wounded in hospitals, attending military parades, inspecting troops and conferring decorations. He made five trips to the trenches in France, where he saw at first hand the kind of conditions in which men were living, suffering and dying for 'King and country'. Seven months after this photograph was taken, King George's horse fell while he was visiting the trenches, and His Majesty fractured his pelvis, afterwards suffering pain for the rest of his life. In March 1918 the King and Queen were back in Reading. The war wounded of course had a visit from their Majesties; eight months on, the Great War was to end. After passing on a cheering word to the hospital patients the royal couple went on to visit Sutton's Seeds, whose head office was in the Market Place. Known across the world, Sutton's were one of the town's main employers, the Queen is seen here greeting the women who worked in the factory *(below)*. It is doubtful that Her Majesty would have seen stoves such as this one around the palace!

'Your Country Needs YOU!' was the message emblazoned everywhere as the first world war got into its stride, and recruitment drives for the armed forces were held in towns and cities up and down the country. Leading the drive for what many called 'cannon fodder' were Lord Curzon and Lord Reading, the noted barrister Rufus Isaacs.

The following year would see Lord Curzon serving in the war cabinet, becoming foreign secretary after the war in 1919. How many of his hearers in this large audience enlisted in one of the services after the stirring speeches of the evening, we wonder? The Great War saw the development of new forces, such as the Royal Flying Corps, which was to become the

Royal Air Force, and new weapons such as the tank.
Shipped to France in crates marked 'water tanks', a clever ploy to confuse the enemy, these armoured vehicles were first used on 15th December at the Battle of the Somme. Their tracks meant that they could travel over terrain that wheeled vehicles could never have crossed, but they were not as reliable as had been hoped because of fuel shortages and mechanical breakdowns.

Events of the 1940s

WHAT'S ON?
In wartime Britain few families were without a wireless set. It was the most popular form of entertainment, and programmes such as ITMA, Music While You Work and Workers' Playtime provided the people with an escape from the harsh realities of bombing raids and ration books. In 1946 the BBC introduced the Light Programme, the Home Service and the Third Programme, which gave audiences a wider choice of listening.

GETTING AROUND
October 1948 saw the production of Britain's first new car designs since before the war. The Morris Minor was destined for fame as one of the most popular family cars, while the four-wheel-drive Land Rover answered the need for a British-made off-road vehicle. The country was deeply in the red, however, because of overseas debts incurred during the war. The post-war export drive that followed meant that British drivers had a long wait for their own new car.

SPORTING CHANCE
American World Heavyweight Boxing Champion Joe Louis, who first took the title back in 1937, ruled the world of boxing during the 1930s and 40s, making a name for himself as unbeatable. Time after time he successfully defended his title against all comers, finally retiring in 1948 after fighting an amazing 25 title bouts throughout his boxing career. Louis died in 1981 at the age of 67.

Both pages: November 11th 1918 saw great rejoicing in Reading when an armistice was signed between the Allies and Germany in 1918, and the first world war came to an end. The euphoria had had time to settle a little, however, by the time the official peace celebrations took place in Reading on 19th July 1919, though the Treaty of Versailles, which concluded the Armistice, had only been signed three weeks previously. The terms of the treaty were very harsh, and David Lloyd George, who was the British Prime Minister at the time, stated prophetically that they were sowing the seeds of a future, even greater conflict.

The finer details of the hard-won peace were not likely to have worried the members of the crowd who gathered outside the Town Hall and along the pavements of Reading to watch the long procession as it passed by. On that momentous Saturday, all that the average person in the street was concerned with is that at last the whole dreadful war was over, the men would be home to stay, and everybody could get on with their lives. All the military services were represented, as were many different organisations, which includes boys who were far too young to fight *(right)*. Wearing full uniform and caps, it is plain to see that they would obviously have loved to have had a go at 'Kaiser Bill'! It is interesting to note that these little chaps were smaller than the detachment of scouts marching behind them!

The Town Hall was elaborately decorated for the occasion, and the Mayor, Alderman S Hayward and his party - all in full ceremonial regalia and medals polished and prominently displayed, were proud to take the salute as the military parade marched past *(below)*.

This page: The streets of Reading were tense with excitement on 25th June 1926, when the Prince of Wales - later King Edward VIII - paid an official visit to the town to open the new Caversham Bridge. Out came the bunting and the Union Jacks, and the people of Reading gave the Prince a warm welcome as he arrived by train. Outside the station, an enormous crowd was waiting to catch a glimpse of the popular man who would one day be their king. A photographer has caught the mood of exhilaration as people old and young sprint after the prince and his fleet of cars as they . moved away from the station *(bottom)*. In passing - most of our readers will remember the fine Pearl Assurance Building and its beautiful terracotta frontage, which was sadly demolished in the 1980s. A great loss to the town.

Yet more people were waiting to watch the Prince perform his main task of the day - declaring the new bridge officially open to traffic *(right)*. The bridge replaced an iron structure which had seen better days, having been in constant use since it was built in the late 1860s. As he unveiled the commemorative plaque on the bridge, his Royal Highness cut a very smart figure with his bowler hat and rolled umbrella; every young woman's heart-throb, the bachelor Prince was at the time deeply attached to Mrs Freda Dudley Ward - who was to be ousted in 1934 by the new flame on his horizon, Mrs Wallis Simpson.

This page: It was 25th June 1926, and the Prince of Wales was in town. The main purpose of his visit was to declare open the new Caversham Bridge, though the many visits, tours and inspections that were packed into his day's itinerary must have made the royal head spin! In Palmer Park, always a popular venue for sporting events, the Prince was treated to this display of physical training put on by teams of enthusiastic schoolgirls, who would have been practising their synchronised movements for many weeks *(below)*. Back in the 1920s, though schools recognised the valuable part played by exercise in keeping children fit and healthy, the exercises they performed were far more orchestrated than today's PE classes, which allow for greater freedom of movement and individuality. Sports of various kinds were also on the agenda, and the Prince and his party watched with interest as boys and girls from local schools took part in races and games *(above)*. The

Prince himself was, of course, a keen sportsman, and he had a very individual taste for sweaters, socks and caps with loud checks, teamed up with natty plus-fours. Lovers of trivia might enjoy reading that one of his lesser known pastimes was needlepoint, which he learned from his mother, Queen Mary, when he was a boy!

The Prince of Wales became King Edward VIII when his father, King George V, died in 1936. The story of his abdication is well known, of course, and the coronation celebrations planned for 12th May 1937 did not go according to the original plan. In the event the monarch being crowned was not Edward VIII, but his younger brother Albert, Duke of York, who became George VI.

The King gave Edward the title Duke of Windsor, and he left England's shores to live abroad, marrying Wallis Simpson the following June. He returned to his native country only a few times during the rest of his life.

Both pages: Ever the perfect gentleman, the Prince of Wales raises his hat politely to the ladies - no doubt causing a number of female hearts to flutter *(top)!* A visit to Huntley & Palmers' biscuit factory was part of the Prince's busy schedule, and this photograph, we are informed, shows his Royal Highness leaving the building after a tour of the works. The ladies in the photograph, however, do look more like a St John Ambulance team than biscuit packers....

An inspection of the Old Grenadiers, a visit to the University, and a tour of Huntley, Boorne and Stevens' works were also on the Prince's list. The company made the tin boxes in which Huntley & Palmers' biscuits were packed - and was especially founded for this very purpose more than a hundred years ago, when Joseph Huntley discovered that the biscuits that he sold loose kept fresher far longer if he kept them in a tin. In a packed day, the Prince of Wales must have been relieved when he could relax over a spot of lunch, taken with the Mayor at the Town Hall. Was this photograph taken after lunch, or before, we wonder *(far left)?* No royal visit would be complete, of course, without a hospital visit, and the red carpet was out for the 'Society Prince' when he called at the Royal Berkshire Hospital. He is pictured here leaving the hospital with the Mayor, The Lord Lieutenant, and Sir Stewart and Lady Abram *(above left).* How pleased and proud those patients must have been who were lucky enough to meet this popular Prince Charming. The Prince (known as David to his family and close friends) was well-liked for his natural charm, and at the time of these photographs there was no foreshadowing of the future events that were to end in a lifetime's exile. When he became King Edward VIII in 1936 he had already made up his mind to marry Wallis Simpson, the American woman he loved. But Mrs Simpson had been divorced twice, the King was Head of the Church of England - and the Church's teaching on divorce was clear. Edward signed the Instrument of Abdication on the 10th December 1936, after being King for only 325 days.

Both pictures: In the 1920s and 30s the Great War was still fresh in the minds of people of Reading, many of whom had lost more than one family member on the field of battle. On Armistice day in 1929, the weather matched the tone of those who gathered for the service in the Market Place - yet the steady downpour did not prevent people turning out in their hundreds to pay their respects *(left)*.

Not too many years previously in a railway carriage in France, Germany had surrendered to the Allies, the Kaiser had abdicated and fled into exile in Holland, and the four-year war had officially ended at the 11th hour of the 11th day of the 11th month. Every year thereafter, a two-minutes' silence was observed at 11am on November 11th out of respect for those whose lives were prematurely ended by the conflict; an appalling total of 8.5 million people were killed in the Great War. The annual two-minutes' silence became a tradition, and across the UK everyday life came to a standstill as people stood respectfully in the street and traffic came to a halt. At the time, the dates 1914 to 1918 stood alone on the war memorial at Forbury Gardens - it was unthinkable that such misery and distress should ever be gone through again. The people who stood in this crowd so long ago had no way of knowing that the future held yet more suffering and loss for the people of Reading.

Armistice Day, 1930, saw yet another gathering in the centre of the town, and even the youngest toddler was brought along to take in the service and learn of the sacrifice made by so many for the sake of their country *(below)*.

Both pictures: *Few who watched or took part in this procession would be likely to forget it in a hurry! It was Sunday 31st July 1927, and a staggering 1,200 members of the Ancient Order of Foresters marched through the streets of the town. Passing St Mary's church, this section of the huge parade consisted of a large number of children. These young-sters could have been members of the Royal Berkshire Juvenile Foresters, who in the 1920s had more than 1,500 members (below). The cloche hats of the little girls and ladies, pulled down low on the forehead, were very typical of the day, while few men and boys would be seen out of doors without a cap or a hat of some kind. The banners of the different courts flew proudly above each of the associated courts of the society as they made their way through the streets to the Wesley Church - in the foreground is the banner of the Court of Robin Hood (right). Estab-lished back in 1878, the Reading District of the Ancient Order of Foresters had fourteen courts within a five-mile radius of the town, each carrying fascinating names such as Whiteknights' Pride, the Merry Men of Sherwood Forest, the Queen Alexandra Court for Females, or the Pride of Robin Hood.*

When the going gets tough, the tough do what they can to help everyone else, and this farm vehicle was obviously what was needed during the floods of March 1947 *(left)*. The winter had been a hard one, with heavy falls of snow that lay for weeks without melting. And then in March came the thaw, and the Thames rose 15 inches, spreading steadily across fields and into residential areas - around 20 streets were turned overnight into waterways. Reading and Caversham were badly affected, and around 1,600 house-holders found themselves in difficulties. For many, punts and boats were the only way to get around. The police were kept busy taking basic items such as bread, soap and coal to stranded people, and often the only way to deliver them was by way of a bucket lowered from a bedroom window! Heating homes was a big problem, as coal cellars and bunkers were of course the first places to be filled with water. People who were able to get into town were at least able to eat a hot meal at lunch time, as the school meals service provided food at the British Restaurant in King's Road. The Mayor, Ald. Mrs Cusden, was not slow to give her practical help, working long hours to provide hot drinks for stranded householders, and later by opening a Flood Distress Fund which by the end of May had reached £12,000.

Like the cavalry to the rescue, no sooner had the flood waters seeped into people's homes than in stepped the Women's Voluntary Service with hot drinks, hot meals and a cheering word of comfort *(above and top)*. The WVS was founded to help people in need, and a large part of their work has always been attending emergencies in peace as well as in wartime. At any time the service has to be ready to cope with full-scale disaster situations, and this involves preparing thousands of cups of tea and huge quantities of food, and setting up emergency rest centres. Her Majesty the Queen paid tribute to the work of the WVS in 1966 by adding 'Royal' to the title. The agency continues to play a vital role in providing care where needed, and the WRVS today provide an average of 350 meals every day for their 'Meals on Wheels' service.

The great floods of 1947 seemed to bring out the best in people. After all, Reading had just battled through the privations of a world war so were ready to cope with whatever the weather threw at them. Wearing a pair of wellies of her own, this 'good Samaritan' is loaning a spare pair to a neighbour stranded indoors *(right)*. Wellington boots were certainly the order of the day - even galoshes were no good with the water level this high!

Remember those rubber galoshes that we used to pull on over our normal shoes to keep them dry? They worked well in moderately wet or snowy weather, but anything over ankle-deep came over the top. Wellingtons were what you needed. It seems that the Duke of Wellington believed in keeping his extremities dry; in addition to bequeathing his name to the Welly he was also an early patron of the umbrella, and his patronage did much to enhance its popularity. Umbrellas were not considered modish until around 1800, but thereafter they became fashion accessories for gentlemen. Indeed, so indispensable were they that

- so the story goes - British officers, while under fire at Bayonne, put their umbrellas up to keep their uniforms dry. A practice the Duke of Wellington put an end to in a message which said that he did 'not approve of the use of umbrellas during the enemy's firing and will not allow gentlemen's sons to make themselves ridiculous in the eyes of the army.'

The flooding was worse, of course, in some areas than in others; under Vastern railway bridge the pedestrians could keep reasonably dry, though vehicles were finding it tough going *(above)*. Few younger readers will recognise the view, which was to change drastically in the mid 1970s when the two bridges were demolished to be replaced by one modern one. It was not only four-wheeled vehicles that had to pick their way carefully through the water - the four-legged also had their difficulties. This runaway cow appears to be making a beeline for the photographer, who would be advised to make a quick move to left or right *(below)!* We can only hope that her minder arrested her flight before she stumbled over some hidden obstacle.

It was a big day for Reading when the Queen came to town to declare officially open the University's Faculty of Letters. Prince Philip accompanied Her Majesty, though there is no sign of him in this happy photograph that records the occasion *(right)*. The Queen, young and pretty, has just received a beautiful bouquet of flowers, and a smile of genuine pleasure lights up her face as she acknowledges the greetings of the Mayor, Councillor A Lockwood, and his party.

Attracted by the pomp and ceremony of the occasion, crowds gathered outside the Town Hall, where the Civic Reception was held, hoping to catch a glimpse of the Queen and the Duke of Edinburgh *(below)*. Full regalia was the order of the day, and the Mayoral party, resplendent in ceremonial fur-trimmed capes

and chains of office, were in themselves a sight worth waiting for. The best view was obviously to be obtained from the upper windows of the nearby buildings, or from the plinth of the statue of the Queen's great-great grandmother, Victoria herself. Elizabeth II had been Queen for only four years when she made this visit to Reading on 22nd March 1957. Unlike her father King George VI, who had been plunged unexpectedly into the kingship for which he had no training, the Queen had begun her training for the throne early, when Edward VIII's abdication in 1936 made her the heir presumptive to the throne. She was only 14 years old when she broadcast messages of encouragement to the children of war-torn Britain, and as the war progressed she gradually took on more and more public duties.

Below: The fame of Huntley & Palmer's delicious biscuits had spread across the world by the middle of the 19th century, in fact - so the story goes - the first Westerner allowed into the palace of the Dalai Lama in Tibet found a tin of good old Huntley and Palmer's. The sight of crates stamped with exotic destinations, therefore, was nothing new in the factory. A special visit from Sir Ofori Atta KBE, however, was a special occasion which called for a commemorative photograph of the distinguished personality and his retinue. No throne was available, but a suitable seat was found for the great man's ample frame, and wearing a benign smile he posed for the camera with members of his retinue - definitely one for the photograph album. Sir Ofori

Atta was Paramount Chief of Akim Akuakwa in the Gold Coast - today Ghana - and the open case of biscuits prominently displayed next to him will soon be en route to Accra. By the end of the 1840s, Huntley & Palmers were exporting their quality products to Africa, China, India, Australia and the USA, and by the turn of the 20th century the company were the biggest employers in Reading. It was a great shock to the town when the biscuit factory eventually closed in 1977.

Events of the 1950s

WHAT'S ON?

Television hit Britain in a big way during the 1950s. Older readers will surely remember 'Double Your Money, Dixon of Dock Green and 'Dragnet' (whose characters' names were changed 'to protect the innocent'). Commercial television was introduced on 22nd September 1955, and Gibbs SR toothpaste were drawn out of the hat to become the first advert to be shown. Many believed adverts to be vulgar, however, and audiences were far less than had been hoped for.

GETTING AROUND

The year 1959 saw the development of the world's first practical air-cushion vehicle - better known to us as the hovercraft. The earliest model was only able to travel at slow speeds over very calm water and was unable to carry more than three passengers. The faster and smoother alternative to the sea ferry quickly caught on, and by the 1970s a 170-ton car-carrying hovercraft service had been introduced across the English Channel.

SPORTING CHANCE

The four-minute mile had remained the record since 1945, and had become regarded as virtually unbreakable. On 6th May 1954, however, Oxford University student Roger Bannister literally ran away with the record, accomplishing the seemingly impossible in three minutes 59.4 seconds. Bannister collapsed at the end of his last amazing lap, even temporarily losing his vision. By the end of the day, however, he had recovered sufficiently to celebrate his achievement in a London night club!

Where success has been brewing for well over two centuries

Late 20th century visitors to the Berkshire Brewery on Imperial Way, Reading, are invariably impressed by the size of the operation, the high-tech plant, the efficiency with which the operation is run and the rigorous quality standards which ensure that every product which leaves the brewery is of prime quality; so just imagine what the Ancient Egyptians would have made of it all. The end product and the basic technique used would not have been altogether unfamiliar to them, as they brewed a beer called heqa from malt or red barley; but it is a safe bet that the quality of beers which come out of the Berkshire Brewery today - national favourites such as Foster's, Foster's Export, Foster's Ice, Miller Pilsner and Kronenbourg 1664 - would have been a revelation to them.

For countless generations, man's love of beer has not only kept the art of brewing alive but inspired him to look for ways to improve the product; and so, after some two centuries' brewing at Reading, the decision was taken in the late 1970s to build a new brewery equipped with all the latest automated plant which would meet the country's increased demand for lager. It was a decision which would have met with wholehearted approval by William Blackall Simonds, the ambitious innovative young man who was responsible for founding the brewery in Reading 200 years ago.

In 1782 William Blackall Simonds inherited a malting and a small brewery from his father. This business, together with a further legacy of £1000, could without a doubt have provided the young man with a very comfortable living for the rest of his life; but William had too much energy and ambition to settle for a life of idle luxury, and he resolved to found a large brewery, with the most up-to-date machinery that the industrial revolution could provide. So he acquired an extensive site in Seven Bridges Street (now Bridge Street) and began making plans. Sir John Soane, who had risen to fame as the architect of the Bank of England, was a personal friend of William, and agreed to design the brewery; this was in fact the only brewery that Soane ever did design, and although no trace of the

Below: *A horse-drawn dray delivering ale to a public house in the late 19th century.*

buildings remains today the drawings have fortunately been preserved by the Soane Museum in London. It must have been an imposing sight: the brewery house was of a double-fronted Georgian design with Corinthian columns at the front, and a decorative tablet featuring a hop leaf over the front door. There was also a hop-leaf design on the drawing-room wallpaper, and the brewery later adopted this design as their trade mark. Originally the pumping of the water from the brewery wells and the grinding of the malt were powered by a horse-driven wheel, but in 1797, barely a decade after he had commenced production, William had

this replaced by a two hp Boulton & Watt engine. Installed in 1797, this was only the second steam engine to be used in a Berkshire brewery. and it is assumed that the investment was made to improve the quality of Simonds beer production which at the time was below 7,000 barrels a year, and would in itself scarcely have justified this investment; however, the steam from the engine was also used for heating the coppers and cleaning out the barrels and thus improved the quality of Simonds beer. So the tradition of innovation in pursuit of quality was set very early on in the brewery's history.

William was a man of many interests, and when he subsequently decided to concentrate on banking,

Below: *Simonds premises in the early 1900s.*

Above: *A steam powered dray pictured in the early 1900s.* **Right:** *Another view of Simonds Brewery.*

founding his own bank in King Street, which much later became part of Barclays, the brewery was taken over in 1816 by his eldest son Blackall Simonds. By 1839 production had risen to 15,000 barrels a year, and the brewery, now the largest in Reading, had 37 tied houses, of which 12 were in Reading itself. In addition many of the new independent beer houses which did not have their own brewing facilities chose to purchase Simonds beer; and so by building up close links with the local public houses and establishing a strong presence in the area, Blackall Simonds was able to prevent the large London breweries from gaining a foothold in Berkshire.

Amongst the London breweries who were keen to compete in the county market were, ironically, two of the breweries which were eventually to merge with Simonds: the Courage Brewery, established at Horselydown, in Southwark, in 1787, and the former Thrale brewery, also in Southwark, which had been purchased in 1781 by David and Robert Barclay and John Perkins.

John Courage was a shipping agent from Aberdeen, with a successful shipping business on the north bank of the Thames, and his venture into brewing was purely speculative; his interest was sparked off by the sight of so many thriving brewhouses just across the Thames in Southwark, and so he decided to invest of £615 on buying a small beerhouse and setting up in the business himself. Sadly, he died only six years later, but even in this short time the brewery had become so successful that the family had come to regard it as their livelihood, and Horselydown as their home. John left a widow, Harriot, and a young family, of whom the eldest was a three-year-old boy, also called John. Harriot Courage survived her husband by only a few years, during which time she ran the brewery with the help of John Donaldson, the managing clerk; after her death John Donaldson became a partner in the business and took over both the running of the brewery and the care of the children. Young John Courage began learning the skills of the brewer at the age of 14, and became a partner in 1811 when he reached 21. Following John Donaldson's retirement 25 years later, John Courage took his two elder sons John and Robert into the partnership, and the brewery remained a family business until April 1888, when the limited company of Courage & Co was formed. In just a hundred and one years the Courage family had

built the business up from one small beerhouse to a giant concern occupying a greatly extended site, with almost 80 splendid horses, 35 vans and a steam lift which conveyed 1,000 quarters of malt a day from the barges to the top floor of the malthouse. Alfred Barnard, in his contemporary account of 'Noted Breweries', reckoned Horselydown to be the busiest brewery of its size in London, with some 1,600 barrels a day leaving the premises.

Left and below: *The Prince of Wales' visit to the brewery in June 1926.*

Disaster struck Horselydown in 1891 when a fire burned the entire establishment to the ground. Reconstruction began at once, but in the interim Courage's neighbours Barclay Perkins provided the necessary supplies to enable Courages to fulfil their commitments until they could resume brewing; and this early collaboration between Barclay Perkins and Courage was 64 years prior to the eventual merger of the two firms.

Barclay Perkins' purchase of the Thrale brewery in 1781 had been attended by no less a figure than Dr Samuel Johnson, who was an executor of Thrale and who, according to Boswell, bustled about 'like an Excise man with ink horn and pen'. Thrales had distinguished itself by developing an association with the 18th century intelligentsia, and Dr Johnson himself had resided at the brewery from time to time; various souvenirs of his visits including his chair and a portrait painted by Sir Joshua Reynolds have become part of the common heritage of Scottish Courage. One of Dr Johnson's famous comments on the sale of the brewery was, 'We are not here to sell a parcel of boilers and vats, but the potentiality of growing rich beyond the dreams of avarice' - and this 'potentiality', which was sold for £135,000 (more than twenty times the sum which

Right: An early picture of The Bugle on Friar Street, Reading. Below: The Boar's head in Friar Street is one of the many public houses in the Reading area to sell Simonds ale.

John Courage was to pay for his brewhouse six years later) was soon realised. Statistics from the time show that in 1776 Thrales was the second largest of the London brewers, producing 75,354 barrels a year, as compared to Whitbread's 102,505 barrels; but by 1809 Barclay Perkins was heading the table, with 205,328 barrels.

One of Thrale's best-known brews in the late 18th century was a porter called Intire, and this was exported all over the world. Porter had been invented in 1722 by an East London brewer called Harwood; until this point the three kinds of drink had been ale, beer and 'twopenny'. 'Twopenny' was a superior brew which was often mixed 'half-and-half' or 'two-thirds' with ale or beer, and Harwood's had the brainwave of producing a ready-blended mixture which could be served more quickly. 'Entire', or 'Intire', was an immediate success; because it proved extremely popular with the Shoreditch porters it was nicknamed porter, and London porter played a significant part in the development of the brewing industry in the 18th century and its expansion both within the British Isles and overseas. And expand it did... it was estimated that in 1722 the average beer consumption per head of population was 36 gallons; by the 1770s there were some 100,000 ale houses serving a population of less than 8 million. It is not surprising, therefore, that so many famous breweries should have been established during this period. Another factor of some significance was the canal boom which began in the 1770s. Breweries traditionally favoured riverside locations because river transport was better adapted to bringing in raw materials and taking out the full barrels than was road transport, and so the establishment of new waterway links encouraged breweries to extend their

horizons. Apparently by the end of the 18th century Thrale's Intire was being exported as far afield Russia, Bengall, Sumatra, Sierra Leone and Botany Bay; some little while later, in 1834, Simonds in Reading began to brew a novel kind of beer for export - pale ale. The great advantage of pale ale was that it travelled well, and could survive the six month sail to Victoria, Australia. Pale ale was then brewed for the home market, and was bottled for the first time in 1858; and when the new and somewhat complex Burton Union system of fermentation was introduced into Simonds' brewery in the early 1880s the quality of their pale ale became very high indeed. One explanation given for the general move towards lighter beers around this time is that increased mechanisation of many trades meant that less physical labour was expended, and as a result the thirst which developed by the end of a working day was not so great. In addition to pale ale the firm had launched another light brand, known somewhat mysteriously as SB, and by the 1880s this accounted for over half their total beer sales.

The Reading brewery had expanded tremendously by this time; output in 1871 had reached almost 58,000 barrels, rising to 115,000 barrels by 1885, and its beer and wine store, constructed in the early 70s by one of the founder's direct descendants who was a civil engineer - another Blackall Simonds - had the distinction of being the largest mass concrete building of its day and one of the earliest examples of the use of concrete for such a large industrial building. The firm's innovative approach was much in evidence inside the brewery as well; as well as introducing improved production techniques, a laboratory was set up under a trained chemist to analyse the raw materials and each brew of beer. They also had great success in finding new outlets. In 1872 they were awarded a contract to supply the garrison which had been set up in nearby Aldershot in the 1850s, and this led to branches being set up purely to supply the army: by 1881 they had ten branches in England, and branches in Malta, Gibralter and Cairo. Around this time too Simonds

Top left: A cooper making oak barrels.
Top right: Staff outside Simonds office in Cairo.

merged with Barclay, Perkins & Company Limited to form Courage & Barclay Limited, controlling some 2,500 tied houses as well as extensive free trade interests.

In parallel, H & G Simonds Limited had likewise increased its holding of tied houses - from 79 in 1871 to 158 in 1896, and to twice as many again by 1916 - and had then, likewise, begun acquiring other breweries. The management of the company had remained in the hands of the Simonds family. Frederick Adolphus Simonds, known as Eric, who was a director and subsequently chairman between 1914 and 1953, and was in fact the last family chairman. He was chiefly responsible for the company's programme of acquisitions. Between 1919 and 1939 these included breweries in Devonport, Bristol, Staines, Cirencester, Brixham, Bridgend and

won the contract to supply railway refreshment rooms for both the South-Eastern Railway which went from London Bridge to Kent and the South-Western Railway from Waterloo to Hampshire and Devon, and a number of seaside piers. It was as a result of this tremendous expansion that the Simonds family decided to incorporated the business as a limited company, and this they did in 1885 - just three years before Courage took the same step.

Courage, by this time, had established marketing arrangements with other companies and were selling products such as pale ale brewed elsewhere. Following their own conversion to a limited company, and once they had recovered from the effects of the fire which destroyed their premises in 1891, expansion was rapid. They set up their own production plants outside London; in 1904 they acquired a brewery at Alton, Hampshire, and other acquisitions followed: they moved north of the Thames by taking over the Camden Brewery, then went on to acquire a business in Farnham, Surrey, which brought with it some 200 licensed houses, Noakes Brewery in Bermondsey, East London, the Kidd Brewery in Dartford, Kent, and others. In 1955 Courage

Right: *An aerial view of Reading showing the old brewery on the north bank of the River Kennet.*
Above: *The late Chairman of H & C Simonds, Mr F A Simonds with his Secretary Miss A M Prosser.*

amalgamation of Courage and Scottish & Newcastle Breweries. The latter company was formed in 1960 by the merger of Scottish Breweries and the Newcastle Breweries; their history, like that of the Courage group, is the story of a number of successful small breweries which united in order to respond more effectively to market needs. Through this association the Reading brewery is now related to other distinguished brews including Theakston's Bitter and John Smith's Bitter in Yorkshire, Newcastle Brown ale from

Blandford, and closer to home the South Berks Brewery Company Limited at Newbury, so that by the second world war Simonds was one of the leading brewers in the South and West of England and was producing 279,000 barrels. By the time of its merger with Courage & Barclay Limited it had acquired another four sizeable breweries, in Swindon, Plymouth, Newport and Basingstoke, and had over 1,200 licensed houses.

Following the merger the Reading brewery became the headquarters of Courage (Central) Limited, and in the 70s, with demand expected to reach 16,000,000 barrels, the decision was taken to move to a new 100 acre site at Worton Grange. Construction began in July 1976, and the first brew was achieved in November 1979 and full 'on stream' brewing commenced in June 1980. Equipped with the latest plant, located within easy reach of the motorway network and employing a workforce of around 600, the new Reading brewery placed Courage in a position to meet the expected demands of the future.

Since then the trend towards growth and consolidation which had been established in these first two hundred years has continued, culminating in the 1995

Tyne and Wear and Beamish from Cork, Eire - the roots of the oldest company in the group can be traced back to 1749, making 1999 the year of its 250th anniversary celebrations. Of all the beers brewed by the company, it is Foster's, brewed at Reading, which currently records the highest overall UK sales, and it is confidently expected to become the biggest-selling of all beers in the UK by 2000. So William Blackall Simonds' ambition to build a big brewery has been fulfilled in fine style, and the success of brewing at Reading will continue for many generations to come.

Top left: Part of the modern interior of Berkshire Brewery's brewhouse.
Below: The main offices, restaurant and reception suite of the Berkshire Brewery.

Birds eye view

The GWR Station buildings survive today as the Three Guineas pub

Younger readers will find this complex of railway lines, buildings and sidings completely unfamiliar and will have no memory of Reading's two railway stations. This view, dating from 1922, shows both of them: the Southern railway station, from where you would catch your train to Waterloo, and the GWR station, which just creeps into the right edge of the photograph, for trains to Paddington. The Southern station was closed in 1965, while the GWR station building survived and is familiar to us today as the Three Guineas pub. It was a red letter day for Reading when in 1989 the Queen opened the new station with its new up-to-the-minute entrance hall and ticket office. Blagrave Street catches the eye as it leads away from the railway towards the old Town Hall, today the museum, and St Lawrence's church. Towards the right, readers will also spot that other Reading land-mark, the well-muscled Maiwand Lion, in the centre of Forbury Gardens. Designed by George Blackall Simonds, the monument was erected as a memorial to members of the Royal Berkshire Regiment who died in the Afghan Campaign of 1879-80.

The dog-leg of Minster Street is easily recognisable in this 1922 view over the rooftops of Reading; but the homes, pubs, shops and businesses that take up the lower right corner of the photograph were to disappear in the name of progress, and the inhabitants of the little community were scattered far and wide. Many decades on, the Oracle Centre with its department stores, shops, car park, creche, nursery and art gallery was to be built on the site of these buildings.

Fortunately, we can spot a number of landmarks which do still remain today, among them the George Hotel in King Street, Jackson's Department Store, Barclays Bank in King Street, and the Simeon Monument. Sutton's Seeds factory, a major employer in the town until the

company's move to Torquay in 1976, sadly did not make it. It was actually a shortage of labour that eventually hastened the firm's departure, coupled with plans for the new A329(M) motorway, which would cross Suttons' trial seed grounds. It was around the same time that the biscuit factory which had started life in Reading as Huntley & Palmer's also relocated - a major loss of yet another of Reading's historic industries, felt by many across the town.

Events of the 1950s

HOT OFF THE PRESS
The 1950s seemed to be the heyday of spies, and in 1951 the activities of Guy Burgess and Donald Maclean caused a sensation in the country. Both had occupied prominent positions in the Foreign Office, while Burgess had also been a member of MI-6. Recruited by the Russians while at Cambridge University in the 1930s, the traitors provided the Soviets with a huge amount of valuable information. They disappeared in 1951, surfacing in Moscow five years later.

THE WORLD AT LARGE
Plans to develop the economies of member states into one common market came to fruition on 1st January 1958, when the EEC came into operation. The original members were France, Belgium, Luxembourg, The Netherlands, Italy, and West Germany. The Community became highly successful, achieving increased trade and prosperity across Western Europe while at the same time alleviating fear of war which lingered on after the end of World War II. Britain became a member in 1973.

SCIENCE AND DISCOVERY
DNA (deoxyribonucleic acid) was first defined as long ago as 1953, and the effects have been far-reaching. The key discovery was developed over the following years and today DNA fingerprinting has become an accepted part of life. Genetic diseases such as hemophilia and cystic fibrosis have been identified. Criminals are continually detected and brought to justice. Biological drugs have been developed. More controversially, drought and disease-resistant plants have been engineered - and Dolly the sheep has been produced.

A scene to bring the memories flooding back! So many streets and buildings in this view were to disappear during the vast changes that came to the town - not least of them the Inner Distribution Road which would eventually scythe across the lower half of the photograph.

This eagle's eye view dates from 1922, and Oxford Road and Broad Street bisect the picture; the long row of sun blinds shading the windows of McIlroy's well-loved department store - Reading's 'Crystal Palace' - can be easily picked out. Another landmark is Greyfriars church,

to the left of the photograph, which was used as a gaol before the dilapidated building was restored in 1863. A keen eye will pick out the Triangle nearby, which has now disappeared, and the Palace Theatre in Cheapside. Opened in the early years of the 20th century, the theatre was by the 1950s suffering from declining audiences. Some obviously supported live theatre, but there was not enough interest to rescue the Palace from demolition in 1961 - ironically, only a few years before the nation-wide revival of live theatre.

By the 1930s Reading had become a bottleneck for traffic

This aerial shot of Reading in the early 1920s reveals roads that are virtually empty of traffic, at least by today's standards. Unfortunately, the A329 - the old Great West Road ran through the town centre, turning Reading into a bottleneck and bringing chaos by the 1930s. Diverting the road away from the centre did little to ease the situation, and things were to stay much the same until the M4 was opened in 1971. Plans to demolish huge areas of the town and build the Inner Distribution Road met with a storm of opposition, and though the construction of the dual carriageway between Castle Street and Caversham Road went ahead, the next stages of road building ground to a halt and it was 1985 before work on the project resumed. The Caversham Road roundabout was to replace the Triangle, the piece of open land on the left of the picture. At the time of the photograph, McIlroy's, whose impressive building is easily spotted just off centre, was Reading's major department store. The store remained open until 1955, and readers who can remember pleasant shopping hours spent there will still have a soft spot for McIlroy's.

On the move

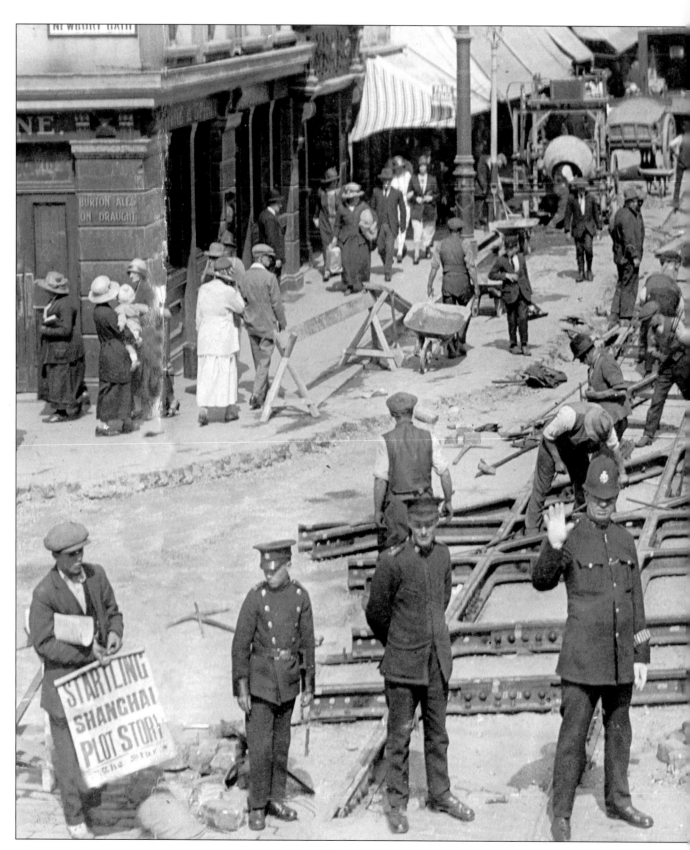

'Come no further!' indicates the police officer - as if one could - and a rather inadequate red warning flag propped up by a pile of granite setts behind him reinforces his authority. The angle of the shot leads us to think that when he recorded this busy scene at the junction of West Street and Broad Street, the photographer had set up his tripod and camera on a tram which has literally reached the end of the line.

The scene is a fascinating mix of pedestrians going about their daily business, picking their way gingerly between barrows, barriers and cement mixers, and workmen getting on with their work on the tram tracks. It would be interesting to pick up the issue of the newspaper being sold by the vendor on the left, and find out just what was the 'Startling Shanghai plot story' it carried - the British newspaper-reading public were obviously as attracted by dramatic headlines as they are today!

The photograph is dated 30th June 1925, and as Reading had had electric trams for more than 20 years at the time this operation was more likely to have involved repair or replacement than the laying of new track.

The upper deck of the tram is crowded on this sunny day back in 1904 - and it won't take readers long to spot that the passengers are 100 per cent male. The driver and conductor - together with all the passers-by in Broad Street - pose for the photograph. Though the camera was by no means in its infancy, few ordinary people had a camera of their own in the early years of the 20th century, and the presence of a photographer still held lots of novelty value.

Reading's first 3ft gauge horse-drawn trams were introduced in 1879 by the Reading Tramway Company, with a service that ran between 'The Bull' in Broad Street and the Barracks, extended the following month to the cemetery. The new form of public transport quickly

Events of the 1950s

MELODY MAKERS

Few teenage girls could resist the blatant sex-appeal of 'Elvis the Pelvis', though their parents were scandalised at the moody Presley's provocatively gyrating hips. The singer took America and Britain by storm with such hits as 'Jailhouse Rock', 'All Shook Up' and 'Blue Suede Shoes'. The rhythms of Bill Haley and his Comets, Buddy Holly, Chuck Berry, and Roy Orbison (who had a phenomenal three-octave voice) turned the 1950s into the Rock 'n' Roll years.

INVENTION AND TECHNOLOGY

Until the late 1950s you did not carry radios around with you. Radios were listened to at home, plugged into a mains socket in every average sitting room. Japan was in the forefront of electronic develop-ments even then, and in 1957 the Japanese company Sony introduced the world's very first all-transistor radio - an item of new technology that was small enough to fit into your pocket. The major consumer product caught on fast - particularly with teenage listeners.

ROYAL WATCH

King George VI's health had been causing problems since 1948, when he developed thrombosis. In 1951 the King - always a heavy smoker - became ill again, and was eventually found to be suffering from lung cancer. His left lung was removed in September of 1951. In January 1952 he waved Princess Elizabeth and Prince Philip off on their tour of Africa; they were never to see him again. The King died on 5th February 1952.

gained popularity, carrying around 14,000 passengers every week, though the upper decks were still open to the elements - imagine how wet and uncomfortable any passengers would be on rainy days! The fleet soon numbered seven, with a total of 31 horses in the stables. The poor condition of many of the horses, however, drew the attention of animal lovers, and was a frequent cause of public complaint.

Below: This fascinating scene of track laying was captured around a hundred years ago - not, as might be assumed, for the old electric trams but for the earlier horse tram service - already well-established at the time of the photograph. With the coming of the Great Western Railway in the middle of the 19th century, Reading expanded quickly, and it was clear that the growing population of the town and the numerous businessmen and visitors needed some form of public transport. It was down to a group of local innkeepers to put their heads together and come up with the idea for a horsebus which would run from their own hotels. But American inventor George Train had an even better idea - lay down sets of rails for the vehicles to run on, and in 1860 Birkenhead in Merseyside became the first town, not just in Britain but in Europe, to run the new horse trams. In April 1879 the first section of the two-and-a-half mile line opened between the Barracks and The Bull in Broad Street, followed quickly by the second part of the line, which ran to Cemetery Junction.

Right: To have called the intro-duction of Reading's first electric trams a 'big day' was a serious understatement. Inauguration day, 22nd July 1903, was an occasion that few in the town would have missed, and huge crowds turned out to see the wonderful new vehicles that needed no horses to pull them along the tracks. For the purpose, a new power station had in fact been built in Mill Lane and 30 of the new electric trams were ordered, costing a total of £223,000. Three hundred guests were invited to the special lunch laid on at the Town Hall, after which the Mayoress ceremonially switched on the current at the depot in Mill Lane.

The leading car was driven by the Mayor, Ald. A H Bull, and guests were privileged to be the first to ride the new trams, some of them decorated for the big occasion. Then it was the turn of the general public, who apparently pushed and shoved their way to the front of the queue, so eager were they to take a ride! The new trams, however, still had no windscreens until they began to be introduced around the country in the late 1930s. Drivers were provided with leather aprons as protection from the weather, but we can imagine what a comfortless job tram driving would have been in a harsh winter!

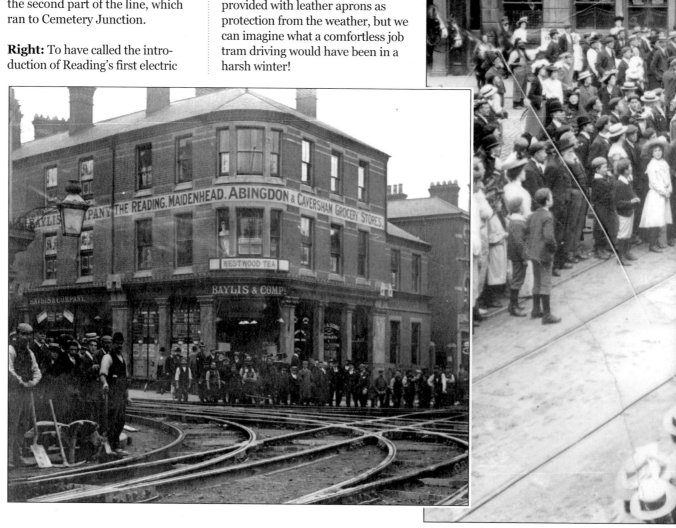

Right: Traditionally, British men have been regarded as the bread winners, going out to work every day to keep their wives and families. Their women folk saw to the children, shopped for food every day, made the meals, cleaned the house, and washed and ironed the family's clothes. The first world war, however, changed the way of life for hundreds of men and women, turning generations of tradition upside down.

When Britain's men were called into military service, women found themselves doing jobs they had never done before, and these enthusiastic young recruits pictured back in 1914 had opted to work as conductresses on Reading's trams. For these girls, hitherto probably dependent on husbands and fathers for their daily finances, it would be the start of a new kind of independent life.

Posters went up everywhere, urging women to 'do their bit', many asking them to learn to make munitions - a risky occupation, yet one which they carried out very efficiently. Many others worked in machine shops and engineering factories, doing the kind of work that had always been looked on as 'jobs for the men'. They did the job, and they did it well.

Below: As it was the Mayor of Reading who got to drive the very first electric tram in the town, so it was the Mayor, Cllr WEC McIlroy, who took the controls of Reading's last tram, car number 13, as it left Broad Street for the depot on Saturday 20th May 1939.

A huge number of people turned out to say farewell before the old vehicles were sent on their way to that great tram shed in the sky, and the strains of 'Auld Lang Syne' followed the last tram as it set off on its final journey. That last tram would no doubt have had its souvenir hunters, who took away with them everything they could lay their hands on, even if it *was* nailed down! Some of the cars were to survive for a number of years as summer houses and garden sheds. How many of the crews' uniform jackets, destination blinds, lamps, handrails and honesty boxes removed from the last trams are still tucked away, half forgotten, in boxes in lofts around Reading? All those guilty, wave your tram drivers' caps....

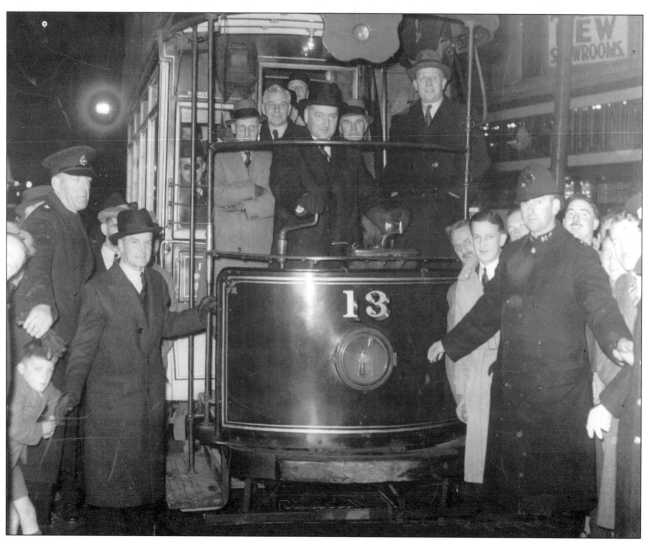

old tramcars were fully enclosed and comfortable.

The trolley buses were to be with us until 2nd November 1968, and fortunately some of the wonderful old vehicles survived to be sent to the Transport Museum at Sandtoft, near Doncaster - an occasion hailed by the Enthusiasts' Society formed in 1961.

Top: The travelling public had to get used to a whole new way of paying fares when the first one-man operated buses came into service. Letting the good old conductors go, however, was to have a good news/bad news 'swings and round-abouts' effect; the good news - as far as Reading Corporation Transport was concerned - was of course that one man could now do the job of two. The bad news was that it took longer for passengers to board the bus and find a seat - and also there was now only one person to take all the flak from disgruntled or aggressive passengers. However, the new system was adopted and today paying the driver has simply become part of life. This orderly bus queue was caught by a photographer around 1967. This bus on the 31 route seems to have that gleaming 'brand new' look - was this one of the new additions to the fleet? In the mid 1960s buses were being produced with a semi automatic gear box instead of the steering-column mounted preselector that had been common since the late 1940s. The newer breed of buses now had a fluid flywheel which replaced the gear change pedal.

Above: A little detective work has had to be employed to discover the location of this photograph. It is believed to be the roundabout at the junction of Caversham Road and Vastern Road; the York Hotel was number 132 Caversham Road, and more than one of our readers will be sure to recognise the rather smart building to the left of it. The presence of a couple of minis among the traffic helps us to date the view as the early 1960s. At the time, Reading still enjoyed the quiet purr of the trolley buses, and a network of overhead wires guided them through the streets of the town - difficult for younger readers to imagine. The town's first trolley bus was delivered on 14th December 1938, and wonder of wonders, the new vehicles which replaced the picturesque but draughty

Events of the 1960s

WHAT'S ON?

Television comedy came into its own in the 1960s, and many of the shows that were favourites then went on to become classics. 'On the Buses', 'Steptoe and Son', 'Till Death Us Do Part' and 'The Army Game' kept audiences laughing, while the incredible talents of Morecambe and Wise, the wit of Des O'Connor - often the butt of the duo's jokes - and the antics of Benny Hill established them for ever in the nation's affections.

GETTING AROUND

The 2nd March 1969 was a landmark in the history of aviation. The Anglo-French supersonic airliner Concorde took off for the first time from Toulouse in France. Concorde, which can cruise at almost twice the speed of sound, was designed to fly from London to New York in an incredible three hours twenty minutes. The event took place just weeks after the Boeing 747, which can carry 500 passengers to Concorde's modest 100, made its first flight.

SPORTING CHANCE

Wembley Stadium saw scenes of jubilation when on 30th July 1966 England beat West Germany 4-2 in the World Cup. The match, played in a mixture of sunshine and showers, had been a nailbiting experience for players and spectators alike from the very beginning when Germany scored only thirteen minutes into the game. It was Geoff Hurst's two dramatic goals scored in extra time that secured the victory and lifted the cup for England - at last.

The camera captures a sad moment as troops from the 35th Divisional Company, Royal Engineers say goodbye to their wives and families in July 1915.

A forlorn little girl stands in the foreground, too sad to wave as Daddy goes off to war. These new soldiers were on their way to Ripon in Yorkshire for training, and in six months' time they would be in

France, ankle deep in the mud of the trenches. How many of these young men survived the slaughter of Passchendaele and the Somme?

These families would see little of their loved ones before they joined the bitter war; was this perhaps the final goodbye for some of them?

This possibility had to have been uppermost in most of their minds as they saw their menfolk off, and the words 'Take care of yourself, Darling,' would have been often repeated at the scene. Empty words to men who had no idea where they would eventually end up, and who had no control over where an enemy shell or bomb might land.

Shopping spree

Mature trees, hanging baskets, booths and benches where shoppers can rest their weary feet are part of this same view today, and pedestrians no longer have to take their lives in their hands to cross from one side of the road to the other. Some of us might miss the kind of scene recorded here, but parents pushing buggies and with toddlers in tow are particularly grateful for the safety of those of our streets that have become traffic free.

Broad Street was busy with both shoppers and traffic at the time of this photograph, which dates from 1947.

By this time, cars which had been laid up for the duration of the war between 1939 and 1945 were back on the streets again, though petrol was still rationed. Motorists had a further three years to wait until rationing was lifted on 26th May 1950. The low building after Burtons, on the left of Broad Street, marks the end of Chain Street - a name which visitors to Reading find intriguing. Apparently, so many delivery vehicles were using the narrow lane that it became congested, leading the authorities to erect a chain at each end.

Right: The shady hats with dainty flowers and long, sweeping skirts worn by these ladies were the typical feminine fashion of the day when this fascinating Broad Street scene was recorded for posterity in 1919.

cinema for the last time, and became Vincents' showroom then the Cadena Cafe.

Below: True nostalgia lies in this busy view of Broad Street, and the young mums with their toddlers and

No sign here of the jeans, shirts, trainers and unisex clothing that were as yet far in the future!

A huge sign outside the Grand informs us that 'The Doctor's Crime' was being screened that day. This would have been a silent film, accompanied by a pianist, or possibly, as in West's Picture Palace and other cinemas in the town, a small orchestra, playing music which appropriately followed the pathos, suspense or excitement of the film. The Grand, which opened in 1911, unfortunately did not live on to see the advent of the 'talkies' in 1929 - the wonder technology of the day. In many places, special trains were laid on to take cinemagoers to shed romantic tears over Jolson's rendering of 'Danny Boy' in 'The Singing Fool'. 'Danny Boy' was of course destined to become everyone's favourite song! In 1922 The Grand closed its doors as a

old-style prams, and the rows of sit-up-and-beg vehicles confirm 1947 as the date of the photograph. Those were the days when trolley buses, smart in their crimson and cream livery, took us through the streets of Reading in near silence. Trolley buses - known by many as 'trackless trams' - stayed with us for 32 years, and the occasion was bitter-sweet for the large crowds who bought tickets to ride the very last trolley bus. The tickets - maroon in colour - for the final tour of Reading on 2nd November 1968 cost six shillings and four shillings (30p and 20p in today's money, though not in value!), and the sentiment expressed was 'The silent trolley is no more, now only the diesels roar'. Very apt. There was no shadow of the Oracle Shopping Centre, opened in 1999, when this view was caught on camera. The George Hotel, however, remains much as it was and is still a popular town centre venue.

Maypole, a well-known chain of shops that once covered the country - surely affected by the growing trend towards self service shopping which began at the end of the 1950s. Sixty or so years on from the date of the photograph, the Cheltenham & Gloucester Building Society was to stand on this spot.

Top: Tramlines follow the gentle curve of Broad Street past Wellsteeds, for many years one of Reading's leading department stores, in this view which dates from around 1910. This impressive statue of prominent Victorian citizen George Palmer stood in Broad Street for many years, though at the time of this photo-graph the statue lacked its iron railings. It was moved to Palmer Park during the street-widening scheme of the 1950s.

Above: This fascinating view of the Broad Street and West Street crossroads dates from the 1930s, when McIlroy's department store was still Reading's Crystal Palace. The row of sun blinds that shaded the many windows along its long frontage can be seen in the background - and their clock informs us that it was five minutes to twelve. The shoppers of Reading sorely missed McIlroy's when it closed in 1955 - though its fine first floor plate glass windows can still be seen. On the right of the photograph, a workman appears to be about to spruce up the stonework of the Vine Hotel with a spot of white paint - a mammoth task, one would have wondered. Many readers will remember shopping at the

The building on the far left, at the time the premises of Hounslow & Company, had an interesting history. This was once the home of Sir Francis Walsingham, English statesman and one-time secretary of state. It was through Walsingham's efforts that plans for the Spanish Armada were discovered, though Queen Elizabeth I's gratitude did not extend to financial reward and the great man died in debt. Elizabeth is reported to have stayed in Walsingham's house on her visits to Reading (and to have attended services at St Lawrence's) - though we are unaware of any plaque announcing that 'Queen Elizabeth slept here'! Sadly, the building was later to be demolished.

Architecturally speaking, banks have traditionally been among our finest and most stately buildings. The problem has been in adapting these establishments to our modern banking systems with their cash machines and the 'shopfront' image judged to be so customer friendly. This branch of Lloyds on the far right of the photograph is still Lloyds, and at first glance the beautiful Victorian building would appear to have remained much as it was. Its interior, however, is where the building has suffered most from the trend towards modernisation, and along with most of Reading's other banks its Victorian history was ignored in the 'improvement' schemes, leaving it insipid and without character. A short

distance away the Midland - today of course the HSBC - suffered a similar fate, and its computerised customer service area has been compared to an amusement arcade. This view dates from 1960, when traffic could travel the length of Broad Street. Today, pedestrians can shop in traffic-free safety from the junction with Queen Victoria Street; the branch of Freeman, Hardy & Willis on the corner was to become Instep Sports Shoes.

Events of the 1960s

HOT OFF THE PRESS

Barbed wire, concrete blocks and a wide no-man's-land divided East from West when a reinforced wall was built right across the city of Berlin in 1961. Many East Germans escaped to the West at the eleventh hour, taking with them only the possessions they could carry. The Berlin Wall divided the city - and hundreds of family members and friends - for 28 years until the collapse of Communist rule across Eastern Europe. Who can ever forget those scenes in 1989, when ordinary people themselves began to physically tear down the hated wall?

THE WORLD AT LARGE

'One giant leap for mankind' was taken on 20th July 1969, when Neil Armstrong made history as the first man to set foot on the moon. During the mission he and fellow-astronaut 'Buzz' Aldrin collected rock and soil samples, conducted scientific experiments - and had a lot of fun jumping around in the one-sixth gravity. Twenty-one hours and thirty-seven minutes after their landing they took off again in their lunar module 'Eagle' to rejoin Apollo II which was orbiting above them, proudly leaving the American flag on the Moon's surface.

ROYAL WATCH

Princess Margaret's announcement in 1960 that she was to wed photographer Antony Armstrong-Jones (later Lord Snowdon) brought sighs of relief from her immediate family. Just five years earlier the people of Britain had sympathised as the princess bowed to public and private pressure, ending her relationship with Peter Townsend, Prince Philip's former equerry. The Church (and the Queen, as its Head) frowned on the liaison as Townsend was divorced. Her marriage to Lord Snowdon itself ended in 1978.

At work

Left: Two hours of desperate work from the crews of two fire engines working with four lines of hose, ladders, extensions and fire escapes could not save this building in Southampton Street - and much of the blame lay on the shoulders of those who failed to call the fire brigade when they discovered the fire.

The drama of 21st April 1931 began when a gas ring being used below the stairs on the ground floor set fire to some material. The small fire quickly spread through Miss Norris's haberdashery shop and began the threaten the flats on the upper floors. A carpenter working on the premises helped families upstairs to safety, but flames cut off the escape route before Miss Ivy Hudson, who was ill in bed, could be rescued. Gallant workmen carried out a dramatic rescue from the top of a ladder, and were able to carry Miss Hudson to safety. The families lost all their belongings in the fire, and while the shop premises were covered by insurance, it was an enormous personal disaster for the families living in the flats, none of whom were insured.

Below: Fire hoses snake across the road, and attracted by the drama, hundreds of people of all ages, many of them on bicycles, have gathered in Broad Street to watch the Reading fire brigade at work. The date given for the photograph of a 'Fire at Woolworths Ltd' is 29th August 1922, yet we have been unable to run to earth any further details. We can only trust that nobody was injured in the incident. Here the firemen appear to be damping down the adjoining premises to prevent the fire from spreading further. Woolworths have had a presence in the town for many years, and their original '3d and 6d Stores' were a direct echo of the '5 and 10 cent Stores' that spread in a chain across America at the end of the 19th century. F W Woolworth, who in 1879 opened his first stores selling a wide range of goods at fixed low prices, had a chain of over 1,000 shops in the USA by 1911. With his brother C S Woolworth he later expanded into the UK, Canada and Europe.

> *Between the first world war and 1930 the number of cars on British roads had increased from 200,000 to more than a million*

The first cars had come to Britain in the 1890s, and by the 1920s traffic was becoming a problem. Between the end of World War I and 1930 the number of cars on Britain's roads increased from around 200,000 to more than a million. This was of course only the thin end of the wedge, and it was becoming clear that new roads, wider bridges and new schemes to control traffic would be needed. In 1914 the world's first traffic lights were installed in front of the House of Commons. Caversham Bridge - an iron structure which had spanned the Thames since 1869 - was clearly going to be inadequate to take the growing volume of traffic, and in 1924 work began on the construction of a brand new bridge built almost entirely from ferro-concrete. In fact, the Aberdeen granite used for the parapet walls was the only natural stone in the construction.

This impressive view of Caversham Bridge under construction was probably taken in 1925, and by the spring of 1926 the bridge was ready for the official opening planned for May. The General Strike meant a postponement of the plans, and it was June 25th when the Prince of Wales visited Reading to declare the bridge officially open to traffic.

Events of the 1960s

MELODY MAKERS

The 1960s: those were the days when the talented blues guitarist Jimi Hendrix shot to rock stardom, a youthful Cliff Richard charmed the nation with his 'Congratulations' and Sandie Shaw won the Eurovision Song Contest for Britain with 'Puppet on a String'. It was the combined musical talents of a group of outrageous working-class Liverpool lads, however, who formed the Beatles and took the world by storm with music that ranged from the experimental to ballads such as 'Yesterday'.

INVENTION AND TECHNOLOGY

A major step forward was made in 1960 when the laser was invented. An acronym for Light Amplification by Stimulated Emission of Radiation, the device produces a narrow beam of light that can travel for vast distances and is focused to give enormous power. Laser beams, as well as being able to carry far more information than radio waves, can also be used for surgery, cutting, drilling, welding and scores of other operations.

SCIENCE AND DISCOVERY

When the drug Thalidomide was first developed during the 1950s it was hailed as a wonder drug which would ease the distressing symptoms of pregnancy sickness. By the early 1960s the drug's terrible side effects were being discovered, when more than 3000 babies had been born with severe birth defects. Malformed limbs, defective eyes and faulty intestines were the heart-rending legacy left by Thalidomide.

This page and overleaf: During the second world war the stirrup pump had become a vital piece of equipment for putting out small fires. The floods of 1947 gave the pumps an opportunity to perform a different function: washing away the mud and silt left behind when the water at last drained away *(below)*. A lot of hard work obviously faces the lady and her three helpers before they can get rid of the mess that still lies outside their shop; how much damage was done to the inside, we wonder? This lady has donned slacks for the job; very sensible under the circumstances, though during the 1940s slacks were rarely worn and were still thought by many to be rather daring and even unladylike. The 1920s saw the advent of the pyjama - not night-wear, as the name might suggest, but a highly decorative bell-bottomed trouser. The 'bachelor girl' image was

Boot Repairs

promoted by stars such as Marlene Dietrich , who wore evening trouser suits to promote the image of freedom and equality, but dressing like a man was all the same

frowned upon in certain circles for many years to come. The rueful look on the faces of shopkeepers who had to throw away tons of stock tells us how they felt about the

flood damage *(below)*. Box upon box of tea, butter, fruit and other foodstuffs had to be thrown away, and the settling mud and who knew what else that had risen from the sewers had even spoiled non-food items such as bars of soap. These people would have been clearing up for a very long time!

Under the stony gaze of Queen Victoria, a group of workmen demolish one of the nearby properties. No Fred Dibnah-like blowing up of this building took place in 1929; this demolition appears to have been a rather gentler, few stones at a time procedure.

It's interesting that flat caps (and a bowler?) were the hardest hats on site during this operation, whereas 'No hat, no boots, no job' is the slogan that reflects today's very different attitude to workers' safety. Seventy or so years ago employees undertook many dangerous jobs every day without gauntlets, safety glasses, hard hats or protective clothing of any kind, and reflected very little on the risk factor. In fact, in some occupations it was regarded as being somewhat less than macho to wear protective clothing!

Today, Town Hall Square has changed beyond recognition from what it was at the time of the photograph. The Wheatsheaf Hotel once adjoined the building being demolished, while further along to the right the Post Office - today Yates' Wine Lodge - replaced an earlier hotel. By the end of the 1990s, a popular bookshop was to occupy this corner site.

Castle Street - where both the spirit and the letter of the law are observed...

The premises of Rowberry Morris Solicitors at 17 Castle Street, Reading, are rumoured to be haunted. Fortunately the spirit shows every sign of being benign - and also quite shy, having appeared only once or twice in the last 20 years.

Rowberry Morris moved into this building in the early 1970s, having practised in Reading since 1958 when Gilbert Rowberry, founder of the Gloucester office of the firm, leased 175 Friar Street and placed his elder son Neil Rowberry in charge. The practice remained there for some 15 years, during which time the partnership of Rowberry Morris was formed. The partners then decided to relocate to Castle Street, and were fortunate enough to acquire the very fine but somewhat dilapidated 16th century residence formerly known as Lyndford House.

This substantial Elizabethan property has a fascinating, if slightly confusing, history. Records indicate that during the 19th century it was the Castle public house, Reading's main coaching inn. Its courtyard is believed to have housed a brewery for many years; certainly a brewery operated in Castle Street for some two centuries, from the early 1700s to the end of the 1800s, but the proliferation of public houses along this street - including The Sun Inn, one of the oldest public houses in Reading - have made it a little difficult to trace the precise

location of the brewery over the years. However, by the turn of the 20th century the ownership of Lyndford House, as it was now known, had passed from brewer Hugh Hawkins to Mr Percy Howse, a tree surgeon. It was subsequently put up for auction in 1923, when it was described as an 'Elizabethan Residence' comprising seven bedrooms, two bathrooms, three reception rooms, hall and domestic offices, with 'valuable factory premises' and various other outbuildings to the rear.

At some stage over the next 50 years it fell into neglect, but was then acquired by Rowberry Morris, who embarked on an extensive programme of renovation before moving in. The attractive frontage to Castle Street will be familiar to most readers, as may the old chimneys which crown the roof. Inside, interesting features include many original beams, one of which clearly bears a workman's trademark in the shape of a shoe . . . or is it the footprint of that elusive, restless spirit?

Left: *17 Castle Street, the home of Rowberry Morris since the early 1970s.*
Above: *Senior partners Anthony Rowberry and Richard Leathem.*

Haslams - surveying the scene from 1838 and on into the future

Pride of place amongst the Chartered Surveyors and Estate Agents in Reading must go to Haslams. With more than a century and a half of experience to draw from, it looks fondly at its past achievements. However, it is to the future that it dedicates all its energies today. Established as a leader in all aspects of residential and commercial property, Haslams' standing in the town was emphasised by its recent handling of the high profile and well publicised sale of Elm Park, the home of Reading Football Club for over 100 years. The site was sold to Barratt Homes for residential development.

It is a sign of the times and a feature in the ambitions and growth of Haslams that it now casts its net over a wider geographical area. At one time the focus was on the land and property interests held by its clients across Reading and Berkshire. A shift in emphasis has seen that balance tilt. An emerging client list includes businesses and private clients with interests all over the UK. To this end it is not surprising to now find that the practice has a well resourced IT system within its offices which are situated in what some refer to as England's 'silicon chip valley'. Haslams has its own website and there can now be no barriers with access to the world wide web via the internet.

This expansion to a wider client source started in the early 1980s. For example a restaurant in the City of London favoured Haslams with instructions to project manage its refurbishment, a Brighton site was valued for the proposed development of over 100 housing units, advice was offered for an office refurbishment in Bedford and the sale of a 26-acre site in the Isle of Wight was undertaken. Even further afield, Haslams was consulted about a school valuation in Newcastle, a warehouse rent review in Liverpool, the sale of a Darlington retail parade and a rating appeal on a fast food outlet in Plymouth.

This is an owner led business that has a comprehensive knowledge of the Thames Valley property market, but became ready to take that expertise further from the home door, whilst retaining its focus on specific customer needs. Although Haslams operates from a single building, it has a large team of Surveyors and Agents with support staff who have skills in all aspects of commercial property, residential property and land. As well as delivering a quality service, Haslams still prides itself on being able to provide the personal touch that individual attention can give.

In its commercial property and land transaction services, Haslams deals with the sales and lettings of factories, offices and shops. Information is gathered and analysed to assist in development and investment appraisals. The sale of a large office development here in Reading, the disposal of shops in Birmingham and the letting of a 17,000 sq ft office in Wokingham are the sort of commercial undertakings with which Haslams is having more and more dealings. Unfortunately, in business, not every company is making millions. Whether because of mismanagement, a recession or sheer bad luck, some firms go to the wall. When the liquidator and receiver move in, Haslams frequently provide debt recovery advice, valuation and compensation reports.

Important development projects have led to Haslams being charged on behalf of clients to steer development proposals through the planning system. An example includes the proposed new settlement south of Reading where Haslams is acting on behalf of Reading University - a client of the firm since 1924. As environment agencies become ever watchful of schemes to alter the outlook and nature of their surroundings, it becomes even more important to have the seasoned professional alongside to guide the passage of

Top left: *James Haslam who, along with his brother Charles, set up the firm in 1838.* **Above:** *An advertisement for an auction in 1846.*

planning applications and appeals to a successful conclusion. Haslams has that know-how.

With its hopes and plans for expansion into becoming the dominant surveying and agency practice in the Thames Valley, the practice has kept most of its long established clients on board. Good relationships with such important bodies as Reading University and the Palmer trustees, of Huntley & Palmer biscuit fame, have been warmly maintained.

Even when the firm first began, it was established as a broad based professional practice from the onset. The very first dealings were in land compensation. The brothers James and Charles Haslam, who had started off as farmers, set up

Left: Dryland Haslam Junior. **Below:** *The firm's office at Friar Street Chambers, pictured in 1958.*

a partnership in 1838. They advised the local farming community on land valuation and the value of their agricultural goods and chattels. At around that time the Great Western Railway had arrived in Reading. Great swathes of land were up for compulsory purchase, as authorised by a Private Act of Parliament. The Haslam brothers advised their neighbours in pursuit of compensation claims for the land and equipment that had been made redundant by the spread of the rail tracks.

The brothers set up their offices in Whitley Wood, in 1838, but soon moved to 107 Broad Street in the town centre. This is now the home of the Heelas (John Lewis) department store. It was not long before they were on the move once again. In the mid 1840s the partnership was to be found at 17 Friar Street. One of the major projects during this era was the design of Amersham Hall School for Boys. Built in 1860, it is now the Queen Anne Girls' School. At that time the company was known as Haslam and Buckland, but Mr Buckland left to start his own firm in 1865. It was then that the next generation of the Haslam family became a partner.

Dryland Haslam's inclusion saw the company name change to recognise his involvement. It was now known as Haslam & Son.

In the 1880s a site opposite the partnership's premises became available. Dryland's brother, who was an architect, designed a purpose built building ideal for estate agents and surveyors on the ground floor, with upper offices taken by a solicitors' firm (Brain & Brain) and the local Conservative Club. The building was known as The Chambers at 156 Friar Street and Haslams has continued to occupy this site ever since. Rooms to the rear were used as the local auction house and also by the Reading Chamber of Commerce. The Chamber used the room as its headquarters until 1945. More recently Haslams acquired the adjoining building (No 155) to accommodate the growing practice. Dryland Haslam was an important figure in the history of

*Above: Offices in Reading for which Haslams undertook the valuation and letting. **Below:** Haslams handled the sale of Elm Park for residential development on behalf of Reading Football Club plc.*

Holybrook development behind Castle Hill for the Council and the Potteries estate at Tilehurst. In fact Haslams has acted for all of Reading's original three Bs, bulbs, bricks and biscuits. These were represented by Sutton's Seeds, Collier's Brickworks and Huntley & Palmer. A new B was added sometime later in the shape of the beer of Simmond's Brewery now Scottish Newcastle.

The history makes fine reading, but it is to the next century that the owners now turn their gaze. This growing business is increasingly engaged in building design and construction surveying as well as its more traditional agency tasks. The administration of building contracts and the overseeing of conversions and refurbishments will occupy Haslams' building surveyors for many years to come. Haslams can also provide expert witnesses in property disputes that end up in the courts. As we become more ready as a nation to follow the American example of taking legal action over matters that may once have been ignored or resolved outside the courtroom, it becomes more and more important to have the best advice and support available.

An expanding client list can be found in the education sector. Across the region, as schools have gained greater budgetary freedom, all sectors from nursery schools to the University have had a need for independent and competent property advice. Wellington College in Crowthorne and Bearwood College in Wokingham are notable clients. Local authorities, housing associations, registered charities and sports clubs are part of a varied client portfolio and even the church and other religious bodies have seen fit to consult Reading's premier property firm.

the firm. He had been a director of the Reading Building Society and the Reading Gas Company. He kept the offices lit by gaslight until the start of World War II. It was only when the Gas Board fitted electric light in its own premises, located next door, that Dryland changed over as well!

Various partners have come and gone over the years, but the last with a direct link to the original Haslam family was Robin Haslam Mann. He retired in 1989 after over 20 years' service. However, when Keith Walker, Haslams' first building surveyor partner, joined in 1988, it was only then that he discovered that his wife was a distant relative of the family!

Much of the firm's past success has stemmed from its heavy involvement in the sale of large tracts of land, such as the development at Lower Earley, which was sold on behalf of the University, land at Calcot (Beansheaf Farm) and the

For Haslams the future is exciting but its past will always serve as reminder of the firm's long and close association with the town of Reading. The two have expanded greatly over recent years and it is good to report that their current success looks set to continue into the future.

Top: *The assembly, valuation and sale of large-scale residential sites is one of the firm's specialities.*
Above: *These offices in Winnersh were valued by Haslams.*

Woodworking skills which have led to material success

The name Hicks means many things to many people in the Reading area today. To house-hunters and home-owners all over the Thames Valley, Hicks Developments Ltd is synonymous with well-designed, well-built and very desirable new homes. DIY enthusiasts will instantly think of John L Hicks, the long-established Timber and Builders Merchants which caters for every DIY need, while the less DIY-minded will be more interested in the fact that the firm has been providing skilled joinery services since 1958. Those who are themselves involved in the construction industry may well have come across the Hicks Group as a specialist in the construction of churches, schools, hotels, banks, breweries, libraries and other public buildings, either Local Authority or privately-owned. On a quite different note, the Hicks group of companies is also well known for its active participation in local events; John Hicks is Chairman of the Woodley Carnival Committee, as well as being a member of the Rotary Club of Loddon Vale and a committed supporter of local charities, sporting events and other worthy causes. Fans of Reading FC may remember the company's generous sponsorship of the Reading v Tottenham Hotspur fixture in 1988, to mark the tenth anniversary of the first

Right: Founder of the company, John Hicks.
Below: The DIY store pictured in the 1970s.

appearance with the team of their (unrelated) namesake, local legend Martin Hicks. In short, the Hicks family's contribution to the community during the latter part of the 20th century has been immense and varied, and it can all be traced back to the early ambition of John L Hicks - the man who built up the business through his hard work, clear vision, and sheer enthusiasm.

John was born shortly before the second world war. At the age of 15 he embarked on a five-year apprenticeship to a local builder as a carpenter/joiner, and having successfully completed his training period he fitted out his father's garage with the best second-hand equipment and machinery he could get and began working on his own. He worked long hours, dividing his time between his bench in the garage-cum-workshop and

As well as being a craftsman and a businessman, John was now an employer; his first recruit was Brian Witchalls, and a couple of months later they were joined by Glyn Lewis. This marked the beginning of a very long association between the three men; Brian went on to become MD of the joinery division and remained with the company for almost 40 years until his retirement, while at the time of writing Glyn is a site agent for the Group. Another person who has played a very significant role in the development of the business ever since its very early days and today acts as company secretary is, of course, Maureen, then John's girlfriend and now his wife. Living with her parents in Woodley and working full-time as secretary to the director of an insurance company, Maureen still found time to do the company's books, while her shorthand and typing skills kept John's paperwork and correspondence up to date.

By the end of the 60s John had moved a short distance away from the 'temporary' accommodation in Woodley Green to a site close by, where he had permanent planning permission. This is in fact the centre of the company's timber and builders merchants arm today - although long-term customers will recall that the site in its early days bore little comparison to the extensive, well-organised and well-equipped premises which stand there today.

sitework at the large country houses and school which engaged him. He took on as many jobs as he could, working with a small team and subcontracting for larger established building firms; the more jobs he did, the further his reputation spread and the more enquiries he received, and within a couple of years he had moved out of the paternal garage in Woodcote, near Reading, and set up his own small builders yard and joinery workshop in Woodley Green, Woodley. These were classed as temporary premises, although in fact he was to remain there for almost a decade. During this time his business continued to grow, and alongside his joinery contracts he also acted as a supplier of timber and building materials, an activity which grew out of his sound business policy of buying in bulk and then offering his surplus stocks for sale at competitive prices in the local paper.

Little more than a year after the move, extensions which doubled the existing space were carried out and the new shop and office buildings were opened in March 1970, setting a trend for growth and devel-

Above: A new house 1970s style. **Top:** *An exhibition stand in the late 1970s which was held at the Civic Centre Reading.* **Right:** *Advertising on the local bus service.*

opment which was to continue throughout the decade. In the early 70s the structure of the firm was adjusted to reflect its various activities. Alongside the thriving business of John L Hicks Timber and Builders Merchants, Hicks Builders was established as a limited company to deal with all types of construction contracts, while speculative developments were handled by Hicks Developments Limited, set up in 1971. The joinery division was officially formed as a separate Limited Company in 1973, operating as Hicks Joinery Limited under the expert supervision of Brian Witchalls. Then in 1974 John acquired a long-established builders' yard at 15 Headley Road, which provided purpose-built premises for an impressive new Head Office for the company. He then went on to develop the site further to provide office accommodation for the company to lease to tenants; the Parkside Business Park, as it is known, is still owned by the Hicks Group today. This successful pattern was repeated in 1979 when the company took over Harry Russell Limited, another long-established Woodley building company; again the premises were developed into a business park which the Hicks Group still own and leases out to other occupants. Harry Russell Limited subsequently evolved into one of the area's leading Design & Build contractors in the late 80s, thereby establishing the Hicks Group in the newly-developing field of rapid-build high-tech construction, before being sold by the Group in 1993.

A more recent acquisition is Castle Coatings; established as paint finishers in 1981 and now a division of Hicks Joinery Limited, this specialist company provides all kinds of high quality finishes including stove enamelling, metal flake, wood finishing and lacquering, Offshore and Ministry specification

Right: New housing 1990s style. **Below:** *Part of the Timber & Builders Merchants premises late 1990s.*

paints and custom finishes, and will spray anything from a batch of interior doors to a petrol tank for a vintage motorcycle.

The Hicks Group today is a well-established business which provides secure employment for around 80 staff and specialist sub-contractors. At any one time the firm is typically engaged on eight major projects and a number of smaller-scale contracts. In all it's diverse activities, quality and customer service are of paramount importance. The DIY outlet has grown into an impressive 'one-stop home improvement centre'; not only does it offer a comprehensive range of timber and building materials, plumbing fixtures, electrical items and branded tools of all kinds, but it also has spacious showrooms where customers can stroll round the imaginative displays of fully fitted kitchens, bedrooms and bathrooms, examine the very latest designs and, if they wish, take advantage of the free kitchen planning and computer-aided design services to assist them in their choice. Many customers then opt to entrust the fitting and

connected with the trade, including its 1984 initiative of introducing a Guarantee Scheme which all its members were bound to offer to their customers.

The well-deserved success of the Hicks Group is the result of the combined skill, hard work and good business sense of the Hicks family and their loyal workforce. John and Maureen Hicks, as Group Chairman and Company Secretary respectively, have now been joined by their son Steven, who is currently Managing Director of Hicks Developments Limited. The commitment of all the long-standing and loyal staff have contributed to the Group's development and ensured that a thriving business will be handed down to future generations of the family. The Group is looking forward to continuing its success into the next century - and the local community can look forward to the continuation of the many roles which the Hicks family business plays in their lives.

Top left: St Johns Parish Church extenstion. ***Top right:*** Presentation to the Reading footballer, Martin Hicks. ***Below:*** Hicks Group Head Office.

installation to the resident experts, and are amazed how easily their home can be transformed - without going over budget!

The building activities of the company have won architectural acclaim as well as praise from satisfied customers throughout the Thames Valley. One particularly well-received residential project was the very attractive Church Mews development in Woodley Green, an inspired scheme entailing the skillful conversion and extension of a Victorian vicarage to provide accommodation of varying sizes. Church Mews brought the company a whole string of design awards including the prestigious Housing Design Award. Other local schemes include the new residential development at Sonning View, Park Lane, Charvil; Coniston Close off Loddon Bridge Road; Warren View and Garden Mews, and new detached properties in North Woodley, near Sonning Golf Course - and not far from John Hicks' own much-admired Tudor-style residence, designed and built - naturally - by John himself. A little further afield are the prestigious Lowfield House apartments at Caversham, the stylish Alexandra House, comprising 11 luxury apartments, at Ascot. Non-residential projects include the new Library at Woodley, extensions and alterations to St John's, Woodley, the new Baptist Church at Basingstoke, and new school buildings at Ascot.

John Hicks' commitment to quality and good practice within the industry is reflected by his long-term active membership of the Building Employers Confederation, and his appointment as President of the Reading and District Association of that organisation in 1985. The BEC - formerly known as the National Federation of Building Trades Employers - is the largest and most influential national trade organisation representing building employers. Its members are required to adhere to high professional standards, and over the years the Confederation has taken many steps to protect the interests of all those

When is a corner the centre of trade?

One of the features of British cities and towns is that parts of their centres or street corners are not known by their proper names. Locals have either given them nicknames or ones that refer to a trade or business carried out there. Reading is no exception. If you said to your boyfriend, 'I will meet you at the corner of High Street and Kings Road,' he would look puzzled for a moment. Then the penny would drop. 'Oh, you mean Jackson's Corner.' To be a part of the local language is a sure sign of recognition of both longevity and respect. What we all know as the department store began in a small way as a clothiers in High Street. This little shop was the first step on the ladder of the retail world for Edward Jackson. He had lived with his parents in their village shop in Sherfield on Loddon. He had a good grounding in business when he and his brother and sisters helped out in the family shop. It was the togetherness of the family that was important and if jobs needed to be done around the house or behind the counter, then the children would skip school to play

their part. When the time came to leave school, Edward was apprenticed to a pawnbroker. He was with him for three years, but the rewards were poor. He invested what little money he had into the purchase of the High Street shop and, in 1875, started off on his own. As business grew, he could often be seen touring the neighbouring villages in his pony and trap. He called on a five week rota to take orders that local carriers would later deliver. This form of 'travelling service' continued for 100 years.

Edward and his wife lived over the shop, but the volume of trade generated by his efforts, the quality of his goods and the keen prices meant that new premises had to be purchased to cope with the expanding trade. In 1885, the now famous Jackson's Corner establishment was

YOUR BOY'S Holiday Clothing
HEAPS OF AMAZING BARGAINS !

Don't miss this Opportunity !

See Our Windows for the Bargains !

E. JACKSON & SONS
LIMITED,
JACKSONS' CORNER, READING
AND BRANCHES
Telephone · 4249   Telegrams : "Excelsior"

Left: Edward Jackson, company founder.
Above: An early advertisement. Below: The original shop pictured in the 1880s.

Camberley, Henley and Oxford as the family business went from strength to strength. When Jackson's became a limited company, John Jackson, Edward's grand nephew, joined the business. A wholesaler's was established to supply the country shops and , with the need for more space, premises were acquired in Abbey Square, to the rear of the main shop, and across the way on Duke Street Corner. A garage on Thorne Lane was bought to house the fleet of vans used for deliveries and the 'travellers'. Russell's son, Edward, joined his father in the business in the 1940s. Together with his cousin, they developed the textiles, furniture and children's wear departments in Kings Road. Can you remember how amazed you were as a child when you first saw those cash cannisters whizzing to and from the cashier through suction tubes? The cousins installed those and countless schoolchildren have looked agog at them as they were supposed to be trying on their new school uniforms ready for the term ahead.

Edward died in 1993, being succeeded by his widow, Daphne, and Brian Carter, the fourth generation of the Jackson family. Handknitting and crafts departments have replaced the tailoring and wholesale business as the store continues to adapt to meet the changes in fashion and taste to be faced in modern retailing.

as the 'Mecca of the thrifty', trade continued to grow. Before long, new branches were opened in the town along with other outlets in Bracknell and Goring. In his later years he recalled the importance of family and community life that his parents had instilled in him. He involved himself in the public life of Reading, serving twice as the Mayor, in 1905 and 1906. He was elected an Alderman of the Borough in 1920. He is also remembered, along with his brothers and sisters, for providing a new Baptist chapel in his home village.

Edward's sons, Russell and Robert, joined the business after serving apprenticeships with an outfitter. Russell took charge of the outfitting and Robert had responsibility for the off the peg department. For half a century the brothers tried to outdo each other, as brothers often do, each trying to make his department the company flagship. Further out of town branches were opened in

Top: Edward Jackson with some of his colleagues at a party at his house to celebrate the Jubilee of the firm in 1925. Above: The now famous 'Jackson's Corner' pictured at the Coronation in 1953.

Lorry Loads of success

The vehicles of Alan Hadley Limited are a common sight on the Berkshire roads. It was a different story in 1927 when former reporter, Ernest Hadley, founded the company with the purchase of a piece of land in Shinfield. The 1930s were the days of the depression and Jarrow hunger marches on the capital but, with a mixture of solid graft and smart business thinking Ernest made a success of it. He extracted gravel from the land he had bought and began the first of a long series of links with the supply of aggregate to the Reading area.

His first deliveries were made by horse and cart. That must have been a back-breaking and exhausting way to earn a living. It did not take long for the company to grow as a reputation for reliability spread. Ernest was soon to acquire his first motor vehicle and by 1946 Hadley's had a fleet of six lorries. He recognised the need

to speculate to accumulate and invested the profits back into the business as he built up a fleet of wagons that would see him continue to trade right throughout the war. He was also bright enough to realise that if he expanded into new lines of business further growth would be possible. Hadley's produced concrete blocks that were used for a number of developments in the local area, including eight houses in Hyde End Road, Shinfield.

In the 1950s the petrol driven trucks were earning the princely sum of £6 per day. At £1,500 each to buy they hardly bear comparison to the equivalent Hadley lorry you'll see out on the roads today. The post-war years saw further company growth. Such was its reputation that, when the East coast was hit by widespread

Below: *Part of the fleet from the early years.*

Based today at Three Mile Cross, Hadley's has also maintained a highly proficient skip and roll on/off hire service for the last three decades. Whether building an extension, clearing the garden or knocking down a block of flats, a Hadley skip will prove invaluable. Waste is taken to the company's licensed waste transfer station which accepts all industrial and commercial waste, hardcore and concrete for recycling. All non-recyclable material is taken to landfill in the bulk wasteliner.

flooding in 1953, Hadley's was one of the firms sent for to help in the relief effort. Again, two years later, the call went out when railway workers were on strike. Coal was carried all over the country to help both businesses and homes.

Alan Hadley, who joined the firm in 1946 and after whom the company is named, took charge of operations when his uncle retired. He pushed the firm into greater diversification and became involved in earthworks and demolition. On the one hand Hadley's was pulling down old wartime Army barracks and on the other assisting with the building of Reading's Broad Street Mall shopping centre. The company became part of the Claude Fenton Group in 1967 and after Alan Hadley retired in 1978 his place was taken by Eddie Edwards. He knew the business backwards, having begun as a driver's mate in the 1940s. Eddie steered the company through the downturn of the early 1980s, the mid to late 1980s boom and the start of the early 1990s recession. In the early 1990s Fleming & Co was acquired which had an established market for bulk products. As suppliers of specialist sands and rootzone mixes to sportsgrounds such as polo pitches and golf courses, Hadley's was now able to move into yet another business area, with Jean Fleming heading the company as Managing Director.

Hadley's specialise in contaminated land remediation, resolving problems by either bioremediation methods or physical removal of land to approved landfill sites.

The company also runs a commercial vehicle workshop which is staffed by fully trained technicians who service and maintain all of the firm's vehicles as well as providing a maintenance service for many other companies.

Today, Hadley's is a far cry from the one man business that Ernest Hadley developed over 70 years ago, but it continues to be a trustworthy, local firm which the people of Reading rely upon for a friendly, efficient service - they will no doubt continue to do so well into the new millennium.

Top left: *Tonnes of recycled material are produced and delivered every month.*
Left: *Hadley's Bulk Wasteliner out on the road.*
Below: *Hundreds of skips are delivered weekly.*

A history of success set in stone

Reading is home to the stone and marble masonry contractors A F Jones and has been now for nearly a century and a half. By the age of nineteen the founder of the company, William Jones had completed his masonry apprenticeship under Mr Bigglestone of Hereford. Ten years later William arrived in Reading eager to lay the foundations of what was to become A F Jones. The firm was established in Reading's Bedford Road where its main office and premises can still be found today.

As well as founding the company William, who was an orphan, fathered a son and four daughters and so, also founded the Jones family which was essential for the continuity of the firm. Indeed, the generations of Jones's to follow managed and continue to manage what has become a thriving family business.

The present trading name of the firm, A F Jones, was incorporated by William's son, Arthur Frederick Jones, when he inherited the business on his father's death in 1910. By this time Arthur had already accrued 20 years of experience working alongside his father. This and his attendance at university in London ensured that the firm's reputation for skilled craftsmanship was upheld. A F Jones has a complete staff record of employees and wages since 1900.

In these early decades the firm's main business was in construction and headstone carving mainly in churches and other places of worship. At this time the stone was transported from Bath, Portland and York by canal and rail. The Italian marble was imported and brought to Bedford Road by canal from London. Horses and carts were also used to deliver the heavy stone to the

Right: Staff in the 1930s from left; Bill Ware, Harry Taylor, Percy Jemmet and Bill Coffee.
Below: Paul Mann working on a 1m x 1m x 750cm high Octaganal Pinnacle weatheringstone for St Mary's, Wallingford.

firm where the 20 or so employees could work on it. A F Jones made its own unique place in the history of Reading when in the 1920s, they installed an Anderson Grice circular saw, originally with a 42" carborundum blade, and upgraded over the years together with diamond blades the saw was in use until replaced in 1990. Other saws were also installed within this period. The 1920s also saw the purchase of a further premises in Prospect Street, Reading where a display area and workshops were erected for the memorial side of the business. These premises are still in use for stone storage and for undertaking specialist carving projects and other works.

The sudden death of Arthur Frederick Jones in the late 20s marked a turning point in the firm's history. The business was run by Arthur's wife Louisa until their son Alan, who was only 16 when he first joined the firm, took over in 1929. He carried the family business forward in the name of his father, A F Jones and indeed it has not been altered since. To this day A F Jones continues to be a family business. Alan's son

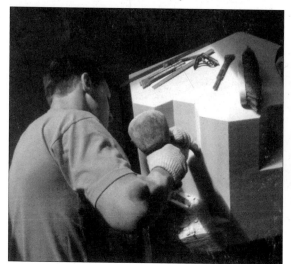

are now architects throughout the South of England. A F Jones now deals in conservation, restoration, constancy and stone cleaning as well as the more traditional trades of carving, repair and construction. Recent examples of these works can still be seen at Reading Bridge which was restored in 1997 by replacing many of the decayed balusters; Reading Town Hall where carved pendants were re-carved and fixed to the niches in 1999; Reading Station where extensive repairs were undertaken to the South elevation canopies in 1998. Also repairs to many local churches including St Mary's Church in the heart of Reading and St Giles' where restoration works to the windows was undertaken in the 1930s. Extensive works to repair bomb damage were carried out to St Lawrence Church, Blandy & Blandy and the Bristol & West Building Society.

In 1996, A F Jones became award winners collecting the National Stone Federation Award for Craftsmanship from His Royal Highness the Duke of Gloucester. Indeed, despite its changes and developments A F Jones continues to strive towards providing the best possible quality products and service drawing from their pool of skilled craftsmen and the knowledge and experience gained over 150 years of work.

Graham A. Jones, MCIOB took over from him and has given the firm over 35 years of his technical experience. In turn his son, Angus Jones, the fifth generation of Jones's is adding to the experience and knowledge built up by the family over the last 150 years with his specialist degree in Construction Management and his diploma in Building Conservation.

A F Jones has continued to develop and expand throughout its history. The war years proved to be the firm's only major difficulty although the business was kept up and running by Barbara Jones and the few employees not away at war fighting for their country. Over the last 150 years the company purchased its original leasehold premises and has continued to expand by purchasing E T Shepherd in 1944 for increased memorial work and a further diversion into funeral directors with the acquisition of Tomalin & Son in 1952.

Today, heavy goods lorries with cranes have replaced the old canal boats and the horses and carts. The main customers for the business

Top left: David Barefield workin on the restoration of Reading Station in 1998. Above left: The completed Reading Station in it's present guise as The Three Guineas Pub. Below: A large piece of stone being lifted into the premises of A F Jones by crane.

The townspeople of Reading gather outside the Town Hall in July 1919 for the official celebrations to commemorate the ending of the first world war.

Acknowledgments

Alan Hankin and Margaret Smith of the Local Studies Department of Reading Central Library. We are grateful to Reading Borough Council and the Central Library for their permission to reproduce images from their collection in this book.

Thanks are also due to
Peggy Burns for penning the editorial text
and Margaret Wakefield and Andrew Mitchell for their copywriting skills.